Accountancy
UNCOVERED

D0228240

Careers Uncovered guides aim to expose the truth about what it's really like to work in a particular field, containing unusual and thought-provoking facts about the profession you are interested in. Written in a lively and accessible style, *Careers Uncovered* guides explore the highs and lows of the career, along with the job opportunities and skills and qualities you will need to help you make your way forward.

Titles in this series include:

Accountancy
UNCOVERED

Jenny Keaveney

2nd edition

Accountancy Uncovered

This second edition published in 2010 by Trotman, an imprint of Crimson Publishing, Westminster Houser, Kew Road, Richmond, Surrey TW9 2ND

Author of this second edition: Jenny Keaveney
Author of the first edition: Adele Cherreson

British Library Cataloguing in Publications Data
A catalogue record for this book is available from the British Library

ISBN: 978-1-84455-199-6

Typeset by RefineCatch Ltd, Bungay, Suffolk

Printed and bound in the UK by Antony Rowe, Chippenham, Wiltshire

Contents

About the author

Jenny Keaveney is a careers adviser at the University of Kent at Canterbury.

Acknowledgements

My particular thanks go to all the people named in the profiles in this book for sharing their experiences of accountancy.

I am also grateful to the following people for their help and advice:

Jeanette Brierley (Ensors); Keith Dugdale (KPMG); John Ellis (SWAT UK); Kay Martinez (PricewaterhouseCoopers); Michelle Mew-Sum and Amrit Saroya (ACCA); Kelly Roberts (Reeves+Neylan LLP); Peter Smith (Quantis Forensic Accountants) for permission to quote from one of his firm's case studies; John Watkins (PKF); Alexa Wilson (CIPFA); Liz, Jessica and Alison at Trotman and my husband, Arthur.

Introduction

Congratulations on picking up this book – you have already shown that you might make a good accountant!

Why? Well, first of all, you've shown that you don't believe everything you hear. It has to be said that the accountancy profession does not exactly have the most glamorous public image. From *Monty Python* to Keith in *The Office*, accountants are generally presented as boring, unimaginative and totally lacking in sex appeal.

So why would anyone want to become one?

It's not just about the money – although accountants can certainly command very good salaries.

Gaining a well-respected professional qualification is one reason many people give for choosing accountancy – but there is still more to a career than that.

Accountancy may offer a higher level of job security than many other careers – but job security is more of an attraction if you actually enjoy your job!

So perhaps it is the range of opportunities that accountancy offers?

Have you a passion? Whether it is for sport, cars, shoes, music, animals, the environment, technology or anything else at all, accountancy could help you to make this passion not just a spare-time interest but part of your working life.

Have you a general interest in a career in the business world without yet being sure exactly how you might put this into practice? Accountancy is one of the best ways to get an insight into all areas of business and what makes a business tick.

Do you want to do something 'worthwhile'? Accountancy is not just about business. Charities, public sector bodies and other not-for-profit organisations all need accountants to help them manage their finances effectively and direct them to the places where they will provide the greatest benefits.

Perhaps you want to work in a 'glamorous' industry, such as film, fashion or travel? An accountancy qualification can help you work at the heart of these highly competitive businesses.

Do you want to run your own business one day? Many accountants do – and those businesses are not just accountancy firms. Accountants own and run restaurants, breweries, nightclubs, record labels, online retailers, technology companies and a whole range of other enterprises.

Are you keen to see the world? Whichever accountancy qualification you choose, you will be able to take it almost anywhere. The largest accountancy firms have offices in over 140 countries. But if you are less adventurous, and want to stay close to your family and friends in your home town, you will find accountants there too!

Do you want to work with people? Accountants don't sit on their own in front of a computer screen all day; they have contact with all kinds of people at all levels.

Do you want flexibility in your career? Accountants work in all kinds of different organisations and it is a career that can fit well around career breaks and part-time working in the longer term.

If you are interested in accountancy as a career, you have already shown that you are not put off by stereotypes, that you don't accept everything at face value, that you have an independent and enquiring mind and that you are willing to investigate your options in detail before making a decision. These are all characteristics that will help you to succeed in an accountancy career.

Accountancy is not an easy career path and as well as the qualities above, you will need to be determined and hard working. It is, though, a career with a great deal to offer and this book aims to give you an idea of these possibilities and help you to take your first steps into accountancy. So now read on and find out more!

Glossary

Accountancy, like any other business, is full of technical terms and sets of initials. This book tries to avoid them as much as possible, but here are some of the ones that couldn't be left out – with explanations

AAT	Association of Accounting Technicians
ACA	a qualified member of the Institute of Chartered Accountants in England and Wales or the Institute of Chartered Accountants in Ireland
ACCA	Association of Chartered Certified Accountants (or a qualified member of this association)
AIA	Association of International Accountants
ATT	Association of Taxation Technicians
Audit	the procedure of tests and checks carried out to ensure that records have been properly kept and that the accounts give a 'true and fair' picture of the financial position of the business
Big Four	the four largest chartered accountancy firms: Deloitte, Ernst & Young, KPMG and PricewaterhouseCoopers
CA	a qualified member of the Institute of Chartered Accountants of Scotland
CAT	Certified Accounting Technician
CFO	Chief Financial Officer
CIMA	Chartered Institute of Management Accountants

CIOT	Chartered Institute of Taxation
CIPFA	Chartered Institute of Public Finance and Accountancy
CR	usually corporate responsibility (the responsibility taken by businesses for the economic, social and environmental impact of their operations), but may also stand for corporate recovery (assisting companies at risk of insolvency to continue in business)
CTA	Chartered Tax Adviser
Firm	the commonly used term for a provider of professional services (such as accountancy or law) structured as a partnership (see below)
FTSE 100	the 100 largest UK companies listed on the London Stock Exchange and listed in the *Financial Times* indexes
GAAP	Generally Accepted Accounting Practice, also known as Generally Accepted Accounting Principles. This is a set of common standards and procedures for accountants in a specific country to use in their work
HMRC	Her Majesty's Revenue & Customs
ICAEW	Institute of Chartered Accountants in England and Wales
ICAI	Institute of Chartered Accountants in Ireland, also known as Chartered Accountants Ireland
ICAS	Institute of Chartered Accountants of Scotland
IFRSs	International Financial Reporting Standards. Like GAAP, these lay down standards and procedures for accountants to work by but, as the name suggests, they are used across a large number of countries

LLP   a limited liability partnership. This offers partners
                     greater protection than a traditional partnership, as
                     they are not personally responsible for the full cost of
                     any debts or other liabilities incurred by the business

Partnership   an arrangement by which two or more people own
                     and run a business, sharing the risks, responsibilities
                     and profits. Most accountancy firms are structured
                     in this way, either as a traditional partnership or as
                     an LLP (see above)

PLC   public limited company. A company owned by its
                     shareholders

PQE   post-qualification experience. Often seen in job ads
                     for qualified accountants

Private practice an accountancy firm providing services to external
                     clients

Public practice an alternative name for private practice; it means
                     exactly the same!

QBE   qualified by experience. This usually refers to
                     someone who has not obtained an accountancy
                     qualification but has built up sufficient expertise in
                     accountancy through their work experience to be
                     useful to employers

SME   small and medium-sized enterprises. As a general
                     rule, businesses with fewer than 50 employees are
                     defined as small, and those with fewer than 250 as
                     medium-sized

SOX   the Sarbanes-Oxley Act 2002, which regulates
                     financial practice and corporate governance.
                     Although this is a piece of American legislation it also
                     applies to foreign companies listed on American
                     stock exchanges

Chapter One
ABOUT ACCOUNTANCY AND ACCOUNTANTS

Accountancy is often thought of as something obscure, complex and inaccessible – a sort of dark art for financial wizards. One of the aims of this book is to demystify accountancy and to show that all kinds of people, from all kinds of backgrounds, can successfully work in this field – and enjoy doing so.

So let's start with some basic questions about accountancy. The answers, though, are not always as straightforward as they might appear!

WHAT IS ACCOUNTANCY?

Accountancy is not just about numbers!

One definition of accountancy, which comes from the American Accountancy Association, is 'the process of identifying, measuring and communicating economic information to permit informed judgements and decisions by users of the information'.

The word 'information' is significant here: the information that lies behind the numbers. This is not readily accessible to non-finance specialists, but they need this information – finance affects all areas of business and is vital for decision making and for the effective running of an organisation. Accountancy is a way of interpreting financial data for users outside the finance function and is often referred to as 'the language of business'.

WHAT IS AN ACCOUNTANT?

If you look up the word 'accountant' in a dictionary, the definition you find is typically something along the lines of: 'a person whose profession is to prepare, keep or audit the financial records of a business company, etc.' (*Chambers Dictionary*).

While these definitions are still true to some extent, they are rather narrow and old-fashioned and do not reflect the range of activities that accountants are involved in today. While accountants do still prepare, maintain and audit (check) financial records, their work also involves analysing and interpreting financial information and using it to provide advice that will help organisations to improve their efficiency, profitability and strategic planning. There are, in fact, several kinds of accountant and understanding their various qualifications, job titles and the work that they actually do will help you to decide on the best career option for you.

WHAT IS A CHARTERED ACCOUNTANT?

The term 'chartered accountant' is often used, inaccurately, by the general public to refer to any qualified accountant, but its meaning is much more specific. There are a number of different professional bodies in the United Kingdom that regulate the training and professional practice of accountants and award their qualifications. Six institutes have a royal charter and qualified members of these institutes can use the word 'chartered' in their title. The qualifications are of a similar standard, but have different titles according to the institute that awards them.

To gain membership of any one of these institutes requires a rigorous qualification process, based on passing professional exams that are generally regarded as being at least equal to degree level, plus a minimum three-year period of practical experience. Chapter 4 sets out this process in more detail.

The six chartered institutes are detailed below.

1 **The Institute of Chartered Accountants in England and Wales (ICAEW):** the largest professional accountancy body in Europe, with over 130,000 members.

2 **The Institute of Chartered Accountants of Scotland (ICAS):** the world's oldest professional body of accountants, ICAS received its royal charter in 1854 and has over 17,600 members.

3 **Chartered Accountants Ireland:** the new brand name of what was formerly (and still is formally) known as the Institute of Chartered Accountants in Ireland (ICAI), Chartered Accountants Ireland represents over 18,000 members in both Northern Ireland and the Irish Republic.

Only qualified members of one of the above three bodies are entitled to use the title 'chartered accountant'.

4 **The Association of Chartered Certified Accountants (ACCA):** the world's largest professional accountancy body, with almost half a million members and students in 170 countries, over 154,000 of them in the UK.

5 **The Chartered Institute of Management Accountants (CIMA):** the world's largest professional body of management accountants, with almost 168,000 members and students in 162 countries, including over 117,000 in the UK.

6 **The Chartered Institute of Public Finance and Accountancy (CIPFA):** the smallest and most specialised of the professional bodies, with almost 14,000 members and 3,000 students working in public sector finance. The majority of these are based in the UK.

Qualified members of ACCA, CIMA and CIPFA can use the word 'chartered' in their title together with their professional specialisation: 'chartered certified accountant', 'chartered management accountant' or 'chartered public finance accountant'.

> ## Chartered accountants worldwide
>
> Apart from the six institutes in the British Isles, there are other
> institutes of chartered accountants throughout the world, which
> award their own chartered accountancy qualifications in the
> countries where they are based. Many of these have reciprocal
> arrangements with the institutes in the UK and Ireland,
> allowing chartered accountants from one country to join the
> corresponding institute in another country.

Not all accountancy qualifications are awarded by a chartered institute:
the Association of Accounting Technicians (AAT), for example, provides
a qualification which can be used in its own right in many roles within
accountancy or as a 'stepping stone' on the path to chartered status.
The Association of International Accountants is an international body
whose qualifications are fully recognised in the UK. It is therefore perfectly
possible to practise as an accountant without chartered status, but this is
regarded as the premier qualification in accountancy.

HOW MANY PEOPLE WORK IN ACCOUNTANCY?

In 2008, the six professional chartered accountancy bodies in the UK
and Ireland had over a quarter of a million members between them,
plus almost 170,000 student members. To this figure can be added
almost 120,000 members and student members of the Association of
Accounting Technicians, giving an approximate total of well over half a

Table 1 Accountants and other occupations

Accountants	547,325
Teachers in state schools	543,326
Doctors	226,095
Lawyers (solicitors and barristers)	151,802
Police officers	136,386

million professional accountants and student accountants. This figure would be even larger if the many people working in accountancy roles with other accountancy-related qualifications or experience were to be included. To put this number in context, here are some approximate figures for other occupations in the UK.

WHAT DO ACCOUNTANTS DO?

Accountants today continue to carry out their 'traditional' function of preparing, maintaining and auditing financial records, but their work may also involve a wide range of other activities, such as:

- ensuring that these records comply with professional accounting standards and with legal requirements

- using financial records to produce reports for clients, managers, shareholders or the general public

- providing professional advice on issues such as tax

- conducting investigations – for example, searching financial records to see if there is any evidence of fraudulent activity

- assisting businesses facing financial difficulties; helping them to resolve these problems where possible and, if not, winding up the company

- assessing the risks facing organisations and helping devise strategies to avoid them or to minimise their impact.

WHERE DO ACCOUNTANTS WORK?

The answer is: almost anywhere! All kinds of organisations need accountants. These employers fall into three main categories.

Accountancy firms

This is where you might expect to find the majority of accountants – but fewer than a quarter of accountants work in these firms. Almost all of them are chartered accountants or chartered certified accountants.

Accountancy firms provide services to external clients – individuals, businesses and not-for-profit organisations. They are usually run as a partnership, owned and managed by a group of partners who are also involved in the day-to-day work of the firm. There are approximately 5,000 accountancy firms in the UK, ranging in size from two partners to several hundred. This area of work is often referred to as 'private practice' or, confusingly and contradictorily, 'public practice' – both terms mean exactly the same. (This book will use the term 'private practice', or simply 'practice'.)

Between them, the Big Four:

- employ over half a million accounting professionals worldwide

- operate in over 140 countries

- have an annual revenue of more than US$100 billion, over $12 billion of which is contributed by the UK firms

- recruit around 6,000 graduate trainees a year in the UK

- audit 99% of the FTSE 100 companies

- have over 2,500 partners in the UK.

The core services offered by firms to their clients are accounting, audit and tax services (see Chapter 3 for details of what these involve). Many firms, though, offer a much wider range of services, often going beyond accountancy itself into general business advice and consultancy services. In fact, the largest accountancy firms often prefer to describe themselves as 'business advisers' or 'professional services firms' rather than 'accountancy firms': accountancy, however, is still at the core of these firms' business and they are leading players in the accountancy profession.

The very largest firms (Deloitte, Ernst & Young, KPMG and PricewaterhouseCoopers) are known as the 'Big Four'. These are actually worldwide networks of member firms operating in different countries according to the law and professional regulations of each country. Typically, only about a quarter of the fee income of these firms comes from audit work, and the other services they offer may include management consultancy, risk management, business development and IT services. Their clients tend to be large businesses (many of them multinational companies), but also include public sector bodies and other large-scale organisations in a variety of sectors.

The 10 firms immediately below the Big Four (in terms of size and fee income) are still large organisations, but they are only around half the size of the Big Four. They typically have between 100 and 200 partners, operate out of a number of offices around the UK and also have international networks. The range of services they provide to clients is similar to that offered by the Big Four but their client range is more diverse, including private individuals and not-for-profit organisations as well as companies of various sizes.

The remainder of the 50 largest firms range in size from 20 to 100 partners and in annual fee income from £10 million to £100 million. Many of these cover one specific geographical region and are a major provider of accountancy and audit services to businesses and private clients in their area.

Next comes a large and diverse group of 'medium-sized' firms, some of these close in size to firms in the top 50 bracket and providing a similar range of services, others with only one or two offices and offering a smaller range of services. Some of these focus on clients in specific sectors, but most are generalists and work across a range of business areas. Their clients are likely to be smaller businesses and to include a larger number of private individuals, often local providers of other professional services, such as medicine or architecture.

The smallest firms are frequently run by only two or three partners: many are sole practices with just a single, self-employed accountant. They concentrate on providing a personal service to small businesses and individuals, often handling all aspects of their financial affairs, from bookkeeping to tax advice.

Industry and commerce

This includes:

- manufacturing industries, making anything from cars to chemicals to confectionery

- service industries: airlines, retailers, software houses

- banks, insurance companies and other financial institutions

- media companies: publishers, broadcasters, film companies, etc.

- advertising and public relations agencies

- sports and leisure: football clubs, travel companies, hotels.

This sector employs chartered accountants, chartered certified accountants and chartered management accountants. Their roles in these organisations may range from maintaining accurate financial records to strategic planning and advising senior management. Their work is more likely to be influenced by the size of the organisation than what products or services it actually makes or provides.

Large organisations will have a substantial finance department that is responsible for preparing accounts on a regular basis and for providing a range of financial information for use throughout the organisation. Many of these companies have a regular intake of accountancy trainees, often as part of a graduate recruitment programme.

Medium-sized employers may only recruit on an occasional basis and are less likely to offer a formal training programme. They may recruit into junior accountancy roles that will provide the work experience required for a professional qualification and will also recruit qualified and experienced accountants.

Smaller businesses may only employ one or two people in an accountancy-related role and will not have a 'department' as such. They will use accountancy firms to provide basic accounting services such as producing a set of accounts or providing advice on finance-related issues.

Even if an organisation has its own finance department, however large it is and however many in-house accountants it employs, it will also make use of the services of accountancy firms. Larger companies are required by law to undergo an annual audit of their finances, carried out by an auditor from an independent firm of accountants. They will also use firms for all kinds of specialised or advisory services, such as advising companies planning to merge with, or take over, another organisation or providing assistance with complex tax issues.

The public and voluntary sectors

Organisations in these sectors include:

- charities

- government departments

- housing associations

- independent public spending 'watchdogs', such as the National Audit Office and the Audit Commission

- local authorities

- NHS trusts

- police forces and probation services

- the armed forces

- the Houses of Parliament and parliamentary bodies

- universities and schools.

Like private sector companies, public sector bodies and other not-for-profit organisations must keep accounts, manage their budgets and produce financial information. Their financial activities are all the more significant when the organisation's income comes from the taxpayer or from voluntary donors and these organisations must undergo independent audits, which may be carried out by firms or by specialist public sector audit bodies.

The work of accountants in public and voluntary bodies is in many ways similar to that of their counterparts in the private sector and it is possible to move between the two sectors. The differences are often more about the culture of the organisation and the factors that motivate the people who work in it rather than the technicalities of the work.

CIPFA

The CIPFA qualification is specific to the public sector, but these organisations also employ large numbers of accountants qualified with the other accountancy institutes.

Anywhere in the world

Over 100,000 members of the six chartered accountancy bodies in the UK are working overseas, according to the Financial Reporting Council. Some of these are permanently resident abroad: others are on a temporary secondment to one of their employer's overseas offices, working short-term in a job they have arranged for themselves, or working for a voluntary organisation such as VSO.

Table 2 Where do qualified accountants work?

	ACCA	CIMA	CIPFA	ICAEW	ICAI	ICAS	Overall
Public practice	29%	2%	3%	31%	33%	29%	24%
Industry and commerce	51%	69%	7%	44%	55%	41%	50%
Public sector	12%	19%	65%	3%	5%	3%	11%
Others (retired, unknown, on a career break, etc.)	8%	10%	25%	22%	7%	27%	15%

Source: Financial Reporting Council, *Key Facts and Trends in the Accounting Profession*, June 2009: www.frc.org.uk//images/uploaded/documents/Final%20 Version%20of%20Seventh%20Edition%20KFAT.pdf. © Financial Reporting Council Ltd (2009). Reproduced with the kind permission of the Financial Reporting Council. All rights reserved.

Employers that may offer you the chance to work abroad at some point in your career include the following.

■ Chartered accountancy firms: the largest have offices in over 140 countries.

■ Other employers in the finance sector, such as banks and insurance companies.

■ Large multinational companies: manufacturers, retailers, technology companies, etc.

■ Companies involved in the transport, travel and tourism industries, such as airlines, shipping companies and holiday companies.

■ International organisations, including inter-governmental bodies such as the European Union institutions and non-governmental organisations such as charities.

Some trainee accountants do get the chance to work abroad, but these are the exceptions – most opportunities come once you have gained a professional qualification and experience in the UK.

Accountants can therefore, as we have seen, be found anywhere and are essential to all kinds of organisation. The rest of this book will take a closer look at the accountancy profession, the different kinds of accountants and the work that they do. In the following chapters you will find out more about the different specialisations, career paths and qualifications in accountancy, hear from individuals working as accountants in a variety of roles, employers and sectors and learn what you need to do to become an accountant and what an accountancy qualification could lead to.

Chapter Two

ACCOUNTANCY TODAY... AND TOMORROW?

Accountancy has changed considerably over the years and is continuing to adapt in response to changes – political, economic, technological and social – in the wider world. These changes affect the way accountants work and train, the skills and knowledge they need, the framework of regulations within which they have to work, and the needs and demands of the organisations that they work for.

Some of the issues that have had a significant impact on the work of accountants in the last few years include: the credit crunch; increased regulation following high-profile accounting scandals in the last 10 years; and the continuing impact of technology on the work of accountants.

KEY TRENDS IN ACCOUNTANCY

Regulation

The accountancy profession has always had to work within a strict framework of regulations and standards in order to protect accountants, their employers and their clients, but accountants today are more closely regulated than ever before.

Background: some notorious accounting scandals

The first decade of the twenty-first century has been a turbulent time for the accountancy profession. Even before the start of the credit crunch, a number of financial scandals involving accountants had brought down major companies and created headlines around the world. Some of the most significant of these are discussed below.

Background to the credit crunch

A 'credit crunch' happens when there is a sharp reduction in the availability of funds for lending. Banks and other financial institutions make fewer loans – whether for mortgages or other loans to businesses or personal customers – and also reduce the amount of money they lend to one another.

In a credit crunch, businesses cannot expand and individuals have less disposable cash, resulting in a vicious circle of reduced consumer spending and lower demand for products. This can then lead to 'recession', defined as a period of negative economic growth.

The recent credit crunch began when banks granted large numbers of mortgage loans to customers who would previously have been seen as 'bad risks'. Attempts to spread the risk taken on these loans by selling on the debt in a package of other loans led to a complex, worldwide network of high-risk debts which, as interest rates rose and house prices fell, caused the collapse of some major financial institutions and brought others to the brink of collapse.

Enron

Enron was the seventh largest company in the USA, involved in power generation and energy trading. In 2001, it filed for bankruptcy and the investigation which followed revealed that the company had been using a number of accounting practices that aimed to show that it was making profits, rather than, as was really the case, substantial losses. The company's auditors, Arthur Andersen, were also put out of business by the scandal.

WorldCom

At the height of its success, this telecommunications company claimed to carry half of the world's internet traffic and emails. As with Enron, false accounts were used to disguise its losses and suggest that the company's profits were actually growing. The fraud was discovered and exposed in 2002 by a small group of internal auditors at the company. Several senior accountants at WorldCom pleaded guilty to charges including fraud and conspiracy.

Parmalat

Italian dairy products company Parmalat became known as 'Parmasplat' or 'Europe's Enron' after it collapsed in 2003 with debts of around £10 billion. The company's founder was eventually convicted of misleading the markets by concealing the state of the company's finances – much of which had been diverted into his private bank accounts in Switzerland and the Cayman Islands. Parmalat survived this crisis and is still in business, having spent a number of years attempting to sue the company's former auditors for their alleged role in the scandal.

The fallout

Following these scandals, a number of measures were introduced to prevent any repetition and to protect shareholders and investors. The greatest impact on the work of accountants comes from the following.

The Sarbanes-Oxley Act, which became law in the USA in 2002. Formally known as the Public Company Accounting Reform and Investor Protection Act, and somewhat less formally known as 'SOX', it introduced tighter regulation of the accounting practices of public companies and their auditors. Its effects, however, have been felt far beyond the USA as the Act also requires foreign companies listed in the USA to comply with this legislation.

International Financial Reporting Standards (IFRSs), which aim to harmonise financial reporting practices and regulation in the global business environment. The use of these standards was made obligatory for all listed companies in the EU by the European Commission in 2005 and they have been adopted by over 80 countries worldwide. IFRSs are complex and, as they become increasingly widespread, accountants are needed to advise organisations on adopting these standards, help to implement them and ensure that they are being adhered to.

Other regulatory bodies and standards, which affect accounting firms, their clients and in-house accountants. In the UK, the Financial Reporting Council, an independent regulator responsible for setting standards for corporate governance and reporting, has been given increased responsibilities with the aim of enforcing 'high quality corporate reporting and auditing, high standards of corporate governance and the integrity, competence and transparency of the accountancy profession'.

These increased levels of regulation and control have created a huge demand for accountants with risk, regulatory and compliance skills and experience, both in-house and in accountancy firms. Clients look to them for guidance through the complex maze of legal and regulatory obligations within which they must now work, and keeping up with legislation in this area takes up a great deal of accountants' time.

Risk management

'Accountants' and 'risk' might not be thought of as a natural word-pairing, but risk is a major growth area in the accountancy profession and it is expected to double in size by 2011.

Risk has been an area of concern to accountancy firms and their clients since the various scandals mentioned above, but it has dramatically increased in importance since the start of the credit crunch in 2008.

Financial risk, from incompetence, inadequate regulation or deliberate fraud, is only one of the risks that face businesses and public sector organisations today. Risk management could be summed up as asking the question, 'What if . . . ?' and it needs to consider all the possible events that might cause problems for an organisation. Some of these events include:

- **technology:** data security, systems failure, etc.

- **operational risks:** breakdown of equipment; transport difficulties

- **personnel:** loss of key personnel through resignation; absence of significant numbers of staff through illness (such as a flu pandemic)

- **political and economic risks:** such as war or revolution in a country that is a major supplier of raw materials to a business

- **disaster management:** fire, flood and other natural disasters

- **compliance:** the risks that might result from failing to act in accordance with legal, professional and other regulations.

Any of these factors could have a major impact on the organisation and its stakeholders. Even if an event has a relatively minor impact on the functioning of the organisation itself, substantial damage can be done to its reputation if it appears to have been unprepared or to have responded ineffectively.

Risk management works to identify and evaluate possible risk factors and the effect that they might have on the organisation. This is followed by the development of strategies to avoid or minimise these risks and contingency plans to respond if any risk should nonetheless become a reality.

Risk management is often referred to as 'business continuity' because it aims to ensure that, whatever goes wrong, the organisation could continue to function with as little disruption as possible in the circumstances.

Accountancy, with its emphasis on testing systems and procedures and its broad coverage of business, provides a good background for risk management. A number of accountancy firms offer risk management services, either providing advice on risk management or auditing the procedures in place. It is also an important part of the work of management accountants, whose role includes assessing risks and developing risk management policies.

Technology

Accountants have always made use of cutting-edge technology, from the abacus and the counting board of ancient times to the nineteenth-century's adding machines and the electronic calculators of the 1960s. Today, accountants and their clients rely heavily on IT systems and software packages to prepare accounting information and to perform the calculations and analyses that will help them use this information to produce reports or to feed into decision making.

Technology is used at all levels, from the most basic, such as using a spreadsheet to record transactions, to highly complex data analysis and forensic investigations. The software used may be generic (Sage being the most widely used) or specially designed for a single, large organisation.

Computers have taken much of the dull, routine work out of accountancy. When the 'number crunching' part of the work – performing calculations and following set procedures – is automated, accountants can not only work more quickly and effectively but also have the ability to analyse financial information in ways that would be impossible without technology. Management accounting functions, such as forecasting and strategic planning, depend just as much on technology as do day-to-day financial accounting tasks such as bookkeeping and accounts preparation.

A 'spreadsheet' was originally exactly that – a large sheet of paper which, when spread out, presented information about income and expenditure at a glance.

Technology also helps accountants working in compliance and risk management to control and check accounting and financial reporting practices in order to comply with the increased legislation in this area.

Outside accountancy, all kinds of organisations, in both the commercial and the public sectors, are also making use of new developments in technology, such as e-commerce and interactive web technologies. These can be applied to everything from buying airline tickets to renewing your car tax, but the security of data and financial information is a major concern for users of these technologies – at both ends! Accountants often advise clients on the potential of IT systems, how they can be best used in the business, the benefits of using them and how any risks involved can be minimised.

One effect of technology is that it is now possible for organisations to 'outsource' a number of their business functions to countries where the skills needed are readily available and costs are lower than in the UK. A wide range of finance and accounting functions, from payroll administration to tax and compliance work, can be outsourced. At first, the work that was outsourced was almost exclusively the most routine tasks, but there is potential for more complex work to follow suit. A sign of this trend was the decision taken in 2008 by Whitbread, the UK's largest hotel and restaurant chain, to sign a five-year contract with the business services company Steria, which will provide Whitbread with a comprehensive finance and accounting service from offshore locations. A survey carried out in 2009 by accountancy software provider E-conomic found that over a quarter of the accountants surveyed believed that they would be sending all their compliance work offshore for processing within the next five years.

Other trends

Islamic finance

In a global market, Islamic finance issues are increasing in importance and some accountancy bodies, such as CIMA and AIA, have introduced qualifications in this subject. These can be taken not only by qualified accountants but by any individual interested in entering this field of work. Since Islamic, or Sharia, law forbids usury (receiving interest on money that has been invested or loaned), accountants have become involved in devising financial structures that comply with this law while being commercially viable. Ethical issues are also important here: not only avoiding investments in activities prohibited to Muslims, such as alcohol and gambling, but also ensuring that money is used in environmentally and socially responsible ways.

Corporate responsibility

These ethical issues are, of course, not solely of concern to the Muslim community, and corporate responsibility (CR) has become increasingly important to businesses in response to a growing public and media interest in the social, ethical and environmental impact of their activities. Eighty-five per cent of FTSE 100 companies mention CR issues in their annual reports, covering areas such as environmental impact, sustainability, community relations, fair trade and human rights.

This may not seem to be very relevant to accountancy: CR can be seen as being 'warm and fluffy stuff', far removed from the cold facts of balance sheets and financial reports, but it is increasingly important to the financial performance of companies as investors demand ethical options and government initiatives, such as the 2008 Climate

Change Act, introduce new regulations and targets. Accountants and their professional bodies are very much involved in designing ways of assessing and reporting this non-financial data so that stakeholders can have quantifiable evidence of an organisation's performance in relation to CR.

Tara is an IFRS accountant with the Carbon Trust.

'I wouldn't have believed it if anyone had told me while I was at university that I would become an accountant! I'd planned to do a master's degree after my BA in Social Psychology, but the course I wanted to do was withdrawn at the last minute, so I went back to see a university careers adviser, who suggested accountancy. I applied to the Big Six firms (as they were then), got two offers and joined Coopers & Lybrand (now PricewaterhouseCoopers) as a trainee chartered accountant.

'I worked in audit at Coopers for about five years in the Retail and Services Group. I did quite a lot of travelling as a couple of my clients were based abroad and I was able to spend some time in the USA.

'I moved into training about two years after I qualified. I was ready to try something new and one of the advantages of working for a big firm is that you have plenty of opportunities available without needing to leave the firm. I was using my accounting knowledge to run introductory courses in audit for new trainees joining the firm, and also ran courses for clients in areas such as bookkeeping and accounts preparation.

'By 2003, though, SOX legislation meant that we were no longer allowed to train our own clients and so the firm had fewer opportunities in training. I didn't want to go back into

audit so I moved into a specialist distribution company.
I found that the working environment in industry is quite
different from that within big firms, which are rather like a
"professional university" with lots of young people – industry is
much more varied.

'I was responsible for internal and external financial reporting
– producing management accounts for directors and financial
accountants, writing press releases and dealing with internal
enquiries. I also worked on ad hoc projects: for example, we
had to convert from UK to International Financial Reporting
Standards (IFRSs), and I ensured that all our financial reporting
complied with the new standards. This involved working
closely with the external auditors.

'I then took a career break to have my children. After this, I
didn't want to return to my old job as the hours were too long
and the work too demanding to combine with a family. My
present role is part time and carries less responsibility but is
ideal for me at the moment.

'The Carbon Trust is a government-funded company which aims
to accelerate the move to a low-carbon economy by providing
business and the public sector with expert advice, finance and
accreditation and stimulating demand for low-carbon products
and services. This makes it an interesting hybrid of public and
private sector.

'My work is essentially office based and I spend a lot of time
on preparing and checking statutory accounts and discussing
accounting issues with my colleagues, including investment
of government funds in low-carbon technologies. I also work
on ad hoc projects: for example, we are currently replacing
our finance system. The Carbon Trust has an office in China,
so my day usually begins with responding to the emails that

have come in from China during the night – these are mainly enquiries about procedures, invoicing and payments.

'The work in industry tends to be more predictable than in audit – a lot of it involves producing month-end and year-end accounts, so you work on a regular cycle. This doesn't mean that it's dull, though – these tasks don't take up the whole of the month or the year in question so there is plenty of time in between them to get involved in other work.

'Training is hard work but you need to look beyond the first three years. Yes, combining work and study is tough, especially if you are working on something that demands "silly hours" (such as a stock exchange flotation) but this is a necessary hurdle. It can be frustrating when you compare your life with that of your friends who have gone into careers that don't require further study, but it will be worth it in the end!'

THE DEMAND FOR ACCOUNTANTS

While several of the issues outlined above have increased demand for accountants, others have had a more negative effect. A survey by CareersinAudit.com in April 2009 found that more than half (59%) of the accountants questioned were worried about losing their job, while 42% of them reported that their firms had made accountants redundant. Some of the largest accountancy firms have asked their staff to reduce their working hours or to take unpaid leave in an effort to avoid redundancies. Even so, redundancies have still taken place in accountancy firms, most of them in the areas most severely affected by the financial crisis, such as corporate finance.

This shouldn't deter you from considering a career in accountancy: even during the recession, employers are continuing to recruit trainee accountants in large numbers and the qualification is versatile enough to withstand fluctuations in the economy. The credit crunch has also brought new opportunities for accountants, particularly in risk management and credit management, as businesses work to avoid the mistakes that led to the crisis. Forensic accountancy is also a growth area during a recession, since financial fraud tends to increase at such times.

A survey carried out by ACCA in January 2009 found that almost two-thirds of chief financial officers, partners and senior finance executives expected demand for qualified accountants to increase over the next five years.

In past recessions, many employers suspended their recruitment of trainees, or made drastic cuts in the numbers of trainees they recruited. This left them short of qualified and experienced staff when the economy improved, and employers today are making every effort to avoid making the same mistake again. Although trainee recruitment has decreased slightly, trainees are still being recruited in significant numbers and some leading employers have actually increased their trainee recruitment.

Accountancy is a career that has been described as recession-proof. Whatever the state of the economy, there is a need for accountants. In prosperous times, they are involved in Stock Exchange flotations, mergers and acquisitions, as new companies are set up and existing ones seek to expand. During a recession, organisations of all kinds need their accountants' advice to make sure that they are using their resources as effectively as possible in difficult times. If a company's financial difficulties become so great that they have to 'call in the receivers', these receivers are frequently accountants who specialise in insolvency work. At all times, the requirement for a continuous flow of financial information keeps accountants busy preparing management accounts, while auditors also have a regular cycle of work. Tax accountants are also in continuous demand – after all, 'nothing is certain in life but death and taxes'.

The following chapter looks at some of these roles and functions in accountancy, what the work of accountants in these specialised areas involves and the experience and qualifications that may help you to get into them.

Chapter Three
ROLES AND SPECIALISATIONS IN ACCOUNTANCY

There is more than one type of accountant. Like the medical or legal professions, accountancy offers a variety of qualifications and job roles at different levels: some specialist and some generalist.

This leads to a confusing number of job roles and qualifications and an even more confusing variety of job titles used to describe them. These titles may refer to the qualification which the accountant has gained ('chartered accountant' or 'certified accountant', for example) or to their principal area of work (such as 'auditor' or 'bookkeeper'). In many cases, people with different qualifications or job titles actually carry out very similar work: the difference may lie in the route they followed to qualification or the preferred terminology of their employer. Some frequently used job titles are noted under the relevant headings in this chapter but it is important, when you come to apply for jobs in accountancy, to look at job descriptions carefully to find out exactly what the work involves.

This chapter gives an overview of the various core roles and some of the specialisations in accountancy: Chapter 4 will look at the initial training and qualifications needed to get into these roles.

Accountancy as a function is generally divided into **financial accounting** – using financial data to provide information – and **management accounting** – using this information to support management decisions.

A number of job roles reflect this division, although others will include elements of each.

FINANCIAL ACCOUNTING

Financial accounting provides the information needed to give a picture of the financial position of an organisation. It also aims to ensure that the finances are being recorded and used in a proper way and that all relevant legislation and controls are being complied with.

The core activities in financial accounting are bookkeeping, accounting and auditing.

Bookkeeping

Bookkeeping is a key function of accountancy, providing the essential information needed to support the work of accountants of all kinds.

Bookkeeping is about record keeping. All organisations need to maintain a comprehensive and accurate record of their financial transactions, such as sales, purchases and salaries, noting how much money was paid or received and who received or paid it. These records must be kept in a format that can be referred to quickly when the information in them is needed for purposes such as monitoring cashflow, preparing accounts and assisting in financial planning.

Double-entry bookkeeping was first described by Luca Pacioli, an Italian monk and a friend of Leonardo da Vinci, in 1494. Although the system had already been in use by Venetian merchants for a considerable period before then, Pacioli brought it to the attention of a wider public and allowed it to spread throughout the world. For this reason, he is often referred to as the 'Father of Accounting'.

Bookkeepers create these records using the long-established technique of double-entry bookkeeping. This involves recording each transaction in two separate accounts, deducting it from the 'debit account' and adding it to the 'credit account' so that the accounts 'balance', or add up to the same total. If they don't, it is immediately obvious that an error has been made somewhere!

The 'books' themselves – the dusty ledgers that so many people still think of when they picture an accountant's office – have long been replaced by spreadsheets, databases and accounting software, but the purpose of bookkeeping remains the same as it was in Pacioli's day: to 'give the trader without delay information as to his assets and his liabilities'.

Although no specific qualifications are required to become a bookkeeper, an understanding of bookkeeping is essential for all accountants and forms part of their basic training. For most accountants, bookkeeping will only make up a small part of their work, but there are a number of jobs that are focused on bookkeeping and support the work of professional accountants. These will be advertised under a wide range of titles, some very general (such as 'accounts assistant', who may carry out other tasks as well as bookkeeping), some simply as 'bookkeeper' and some focused on one specific part of bookkeeping, such as 'purchase ledger' or 'sales ledger'.

A number of further education colleges offer bookkeeping courses and it is also possible to study bookkeeping by distance learning. The Institute of Certified Bookkeepers and the International Association of Bookkeepers award qualifications and details of training providers can be found on their websites.

As well as the technical and computer skills that your training will provide, bookkeeping demands the ability to work accurately and pay close attention to detail, even when dealing with large volumes of work or working to meet deadlines.

Bookkeepers are needed by any organisation that needs to keep accounts – businesses of all kinds and public sector bodies as well as accountancy firms. Many bookkeepers work on a self-employed or freelance basis.

Accounting

Sometimes used interchangeably with 'accountancy', the term 'accounting' has a more specific meaning for accountants. Accounting in this sense refers to the process of creating a summary of the financial transactions in a standardised format, known as a set of accounts. In many organisations, this is carried out on an ongoing basis through good bookkeeping practices, but many small businesses take a more casual approach to their record-keeping and call in an external accountant to sort it out at the end of the financial year. The result of this is the dreaded 'brown paper bag' or 'shoebox' job, when the accountant is presented with an unsorted collection of receipts, invoices and other paperwork and has to use these to produce a nice neat set of accounts or to gather the information needed to complete a tax return.

Trainee accountants and accounting technicians in practice, business or the public sector are likely to be involved in accounting tasks; other job titles to look out for include assistant accountant or finance officer.

Bookkeeping and accounting may be carried out by employees of the company or may be outsourced to specialist providers of these services. Strictly speaking, no qualification is required in order to keep records and produce accounts: auditing, however, is more tightly regulated.

Auditing

Audit is a core activity in accountancy and most chartered and certified accountancy trainees in practice will spend a large part of their time on audit work. This involves checking and testing the accounts to confirm that the records have been properly entered and maintained, that the systems used are functioning as they should and that the accounts give a 'true and fair' picture of the organisation's financial state of affairs. Traditionally, the majority of this work has been 'external audit', but 'internal audit' now makes up a growing volume of work in all kinds of organisations.

External audit

All kinds of organisation – companies, public sector bodies and charities – need to undergo an annual audit by an independent, external auditor. These auditors are employed by chartered or certified accountancy firms, or by a specialist public sector audit body such as the National Audit Office or the Audit Commission.

Audits must be supervised and signed by a suitably qualified accountant (a chartered or certified accountant or member of the AIA) but are usually carried out by a number of accountants, accounting technicians and/or trainees, working as a team.

An audit team works at the client's premises, allowing the auditor access to all areas of the business. They examine the accounting records and check a sample of transactions to ensure that a transaction entered in the accounts is supported by evidence, such as an invoice or receipt. An audit, though, will look beyond the accounts themselves and auditors may need to check stock and other assets, such as buildings or vehicles, to assess the overall value of the company. They talk to staff at all levels of the organisation, from senior management to warehouse staff, to gather the information they need. This process may last a couple of days or a couple of months, depending on the size of the client and the complexity of the audit. Finally, a report of the audit, containing specific items of information and including any relevant comments about the background to these accounts, will be submitted to Companies House and made available to shareholders, the press and interested members of the public.

Auditors don't take anything for granted and you have to check all kinds of details. For example, if the accounts show that the company has purchased a new delivery van we need to carry out a 'fixed asset verification' – physically checking that the van exists, that the company is in possession of the correct registration documents and that the details of the two correspond.

Trainee in a large regional firm

Audit is not simply about accounts: it is about the business as a whole and it relies on information provided by the people who work in that business. A good auditor therefore needs to be able to quickly establish a rapport with all kinds of people but also to be able to gather information from them by asking the right questions in a tactful way, by listening carefully to the answers given and being persistent in their questioning where necessary. He or she must also be able to work accurately under pressure and pay attention to detail.

The audit process aims to provide an assurance that the financial affairs of a company are in good order. For this reason, the term 'assurance' is often used alongside 'audit' by accountancy firms providing this service. Some firms simply have an audit department, others an audit and assurance department and a few call this service simply 'assurance'.

The terminology may vary but the function and the importance of the service is the same, whatever the department providing it is called.

> *Auditing and accountancy are about understanding the client, analysing how they function and what their strategy is. This allows us to really understand the business, and to ensure that the financial statements 'stack up' with what is expected of that business. Managing an audit is a form of project management covering things like planning, goal setting and recruiting the team. The skills you learn are much broader than just learning technical skills.*
>
> *Recently qualified accountant in a large London firm*

Internal audit

All government departments and agencies are required to carry out internal audit and it is widespread in other public sector organisations. Banks, other financial institutions, manufacturing and technology companies, retailers and media organisations also use internal auditors: even though internal audit is not a legal requirement for these organisations, it is a valuable tool in helping them to work as effectively as possible.

Internal audit is less about accounting than about looking at the systems and processes by which an organisation is run, with a particular emphasis on the risks that it might face and the controls in place to prevent them. Like external auditors, internal auditors carry out tests and checks, talk to people throughout the organisation and produce reports. However, these reports, and the information gathered during the audit, will normally remain within the organisation to be used by senior managers and directors. Audit therefore contributes to the management accountancy function.

In spite of its name, internal audit does not have to be carried out by an organisation's own staff – the internal auditors are often employed by accountancy firms or consultants.

Although many accountants who have gained experience in external audit during their training move into internal audit after qualification, it is possible to train in internal audit from the start of your career. Depending on your employer, you could train for any one of the professional accountancy qualifications, as all are potentially relevant. If you are

certain that you want to specialise in this area, you could also study for
the Diploma in Internal Audit Practice offered by the Institute of Internal
Auditors.

MANAGEMENT ACCOUNTING

Management accounting uses financial data to analyse a company's
performance in detail and to provide information that can assist managers
in making business decisions. The work of a management accountant is
described below.

Budgeting and forecasting

Everyone is familiar with the annual Budget presented to Parliament by
the Chancellor of the Exchequer, but all kinds of organisations prepare
budgets for the same purpose – to plan how they will manage their
spending over the forthcoming year.

In large organisations, this involves preparing a number of different
budgets for the various departments and functions that make up the
organisation, so that they can be used by those individual departments
as well as by the organisation as a whole. Budgets can also be used to
plan ahead over a shorter or longer period than the financial year.

Forecasting is used to provide
background information for preparing
budgets and for analysing possible
outcomes of management decisions. All
kinds of data can be involved in these
forecasts – not just sales figures and

> The word **budget**
> comes from **bougette**,
> an old French word
> meaning **little bag**.

profits, but also figures such as the numbers of visitors to a theme park,
operations carried out in a hospital or items donated to a charity.

Reporting

All organisations produce regular financial reports to keep management
up to date with how the organisation is performing in relation to its
budget and targets. Depending on the organisation, these reports
may be produced on a monthly, weekly or quarterly basis: fast-moving
businesses such as retail may even require daily reports.

A key aspect of reporting is variance reporting, which looks at the difference between predicted and actual performance. This helps to pick up discrepancies at an early stage and to analyse the reasons why these discrepancies have occurred.

Reports may also cover non-financial data such as manufacturing output, delivery times and absenteeism.

Advice

The financial reports on their own will be of only limited value to managers outside the finance function. A key part of the role of management accountants is to interpret financial information and use it to provide advice to non-finance managers. The advice and information provided by management accountants plays a vital role in forward planning and decision making by management at all levels throughout the organisation.

Compliance and risk management

As we have seen, the finance function in all types of organisation is subject to increasing regulation and control. While day-to-day compliance with these regulations is more likely to be the responsibility of financial accountants (where these functions are split), management accountants are involved in evaluating financial processes and controls and ensure that they are functioning effectively. They also assess the various financial and business risks that may face the organisation and the effect these could have on its operations and evaluate the costs and benefits of different strategies that could be used to prevent, or mitigate the impact of, these risks.

Project work

This is where management accountants can use their financial skills and business understanding to work outside the narrow confines of the finance function. Projects may be long or short term and can cover a huge variety of activities such as:

■ construction projects

■ developing new IT or reporting systems

■ devising ways for a charity to use its funds more effectively

- evaluating the benefits of switching to alternative energy sources

- seeking ways to respond to changes in the business environment, or

- forming new policies and strategies for the running of the organisation.

Melissa is a management accountant at a record company.

case STUDY

Melissa never planned to become an accountant: after graduating in Management Science and Business Administration she went travelling for a while and then joined a major retail company on their graduate training scheme. This involved placements in a number of different departments in the central finance function.

Although this opened up the possibility of a career in accountancy to Melissa, she didn't feel that she wanted to stay in a large company and follow a traditional graduate scheme. She therefore joined a leading drinks company (one of the Times Top 100 graduate employers) as an assistant management accountant in 2006.

This company, which at that time was only seven years old and had fewer than 70 employees, was quite a different environment from her previous employer. Melissa went from processing invoices to being an integral part of the small accounts team with increasing levels of responsibility. The experience that she gained here helped her to get her current post as a management accountant at a major record label with many well-known artists, a commanding market share and a multitude of global operations.

This may sound like one of the more glamorous roles for an accountant, but Melissa is matter-of-fact about the music business. 'There is a lot of routine work in finance, so wherever you work you follow the same procedures – just because you're working in a "cool" industry doesn't make it any different. Artists do come into the office, but to liaise with marketing or A&R – not finance. Even so, working with a product that you're actually interested in is really motivating and we also get a fair share of CDs and gig tickets!'

Although the company outsources some of the most routine work, such as accounts payable and receivable, there is still the regular round of month-end and year-end accounts which need to be prepared and sent off to the company's head office in New York. Melissa's favourite part of her job is the more analytical project work, where she can use her accounting skills to assess the various income/expenditures for potential new artist signings as well as the financial impact of issues such as increases in digital and merchandising income or decreases in physical CD sales. This often involves working with other departments of the company and gives a good insight into the music business and how finance fits into it.

Melissa's advice to students interested in accountancy is to 'get as much experience as possible. This needn't just be in accountancy firms or departments as knowledge of other areas of any business will be useful. Make sure that you find out as much first-hand information as possible, especially if you do aim to work in a high-profile area such as the music industry. Finally, don't underestimate the amount of time and hard work that it will take to pass the exams!'

Management accountants have traditionally been employed directly by organisations, in business, finance and the public sector, where they can work closely with other departments and build up relationships with managers across the organisation as a whole. However, a number of management accounting functions are increasingly being outsourced to external providers.

Table 3 Differences between financial accounting and management accounting

Financial Accounting	Management Accounting
Provides information to be made available to users outside the organisation through published accounts.	Provides information for internal users.
Produces legally required information in a standardised format covering a set period (normally a financial year).	Produces information according to the demands of the organisation.
Looks back at financial activities that may extend a year or more into the past.	Provides information on recent activity and uses this to plan future activities.
Purpose is to provide a record and comply with legal requirements.	Purpose is to help the organisation as a whole to work effectively.

Financial accounting and management accounting are not mutually exclusive and there is quite a bit of overlap between them. All trainee accountants will gain a grounding in both financial accounting and management accounting through studying for their professional exams. Qualified accountants may cover both aspects of accounting in their day-to-day work: for example, a small company may employ only one accountant who will produce accounting information for both internal and external users. Auditors regularly use the insight that they gain into their clients' business processes to advise them on a range of finance and business issues.

SPECIALISATIONS

Within these two broad types of accounting, and often overlapping the two, are a number of specialised roles, such as tax, insolvency and forensic accounting. Most accountants will only begin to specialise after they qualify, but there are growing opportunities to specialise from the start of your training contract, especially in the large accountancy firms.

Tax

Although taxation can be a specialised career role, it is also an area which just about every accountant will encounter at some stage of their career, wherever they work and whatever they do.

Tax work has elements of both financial and management accounting. An important part of tax work is focused on compliance with tax law, such as preparing annual tax returns that declare the taxable income of an individual or a company. However, since nobody wants to pay more tax than they have to, a considerable amount of tax work involves analysing a client's affairs in order to help them with their tax planning and to advise them how they might minimise the amount of tax they have to pay.

There are different kinds of tax and different kinds of client. The main types of tax are direct and indirect tax.

■ **Direct taxes** are levied on the person or organisation responsible for paying them to the government. These include income tax (the tax that gets deducted from your weekly or monthly payslip), corporation tax (tax paid by businesses on their profits) and inheritance tax, commonly known as 'death duties' (the tax paid on the value of the assets left by a person at their death).

Her Majesty's Revenue & Customs (HMRC) is responsible for collecting both direct and indirect taxes in the UK. HMRC was formed in 2005 from a merger between the Inland Revenue and HM Customs & Excise, which previously had separate responsibilities for collecting direct and indirect taxes.

■ **Indirect taxes** are added to the price paid by customers for a product or service, which the provider must then pay to the government. These include VAT (value added tax) and excise duty (paid on, for example, alcohol, tobacco and petrol).

Many tax specialists work in the tax divisions of general practice accountancy firms; some work in 'boutique' firms that focus exclusively on providing tax advice; and others work in house, within organisations such as companies, banks, law firms and, of course, HMRC.

The clients you might work with as a tax accountant include:

- businesses of all types and sizes

- individuals, ranging from self-employed entrepreneurs and professionals to celebrities and billionaires

- charities and other not-for-profit organisations.

Although personal taxes and business taxes are classed and collected separately, it is not always easy to disentangle the two when you are dealing with the tax affairs of a self-employed individual, or the owner-manager of a small business.

On a day-to-day basis, a tax accountant's work is likely to involve the following.

- Gathering information from clients, developing an understanding of their financial and/or business affairs, checking anything that is unclear or unusual and working out their tax liabilities.

- Preparing tax returns. These are statements of income received and allowances claimed, which must be sent to HMRC by a specific date each year so that HMRC can work out the tax to be paid by an individual or a company. Businesses must also file VAT returns, showing the VAT paid and received by the business for goods and services provided or purchased.

- Advising clients on, for example, changes in tax law and their implications for the client, how to minimise the amount of tax they must pay, the effects of a merger or a relocation abroad on their tax status, setting up trusts to avoid death duties or to benefit their family.

- Liaison with HMRC: in writing, by phone or face to face. This may involve providing HMRC with information on behalf of clients, responding to their queries, assisting clients who are under investigation by HMRC, or appealing at a tribunal against an HMRC decision.

In large firms and organisations, tax often has a strong international element. This may involve assisting the human resources department with tax queries relating to staff on international secondments, ensuring compliance with tax law in multiple jurisdictions and advising on the most advantageous use of an organisation's multinational operations for tax savings.

Tax work is likely to appeal to people who enjoy both problem solving and contact with clients. You will need good analytical skills and attention to detail, but will also need the confidence to be able to give your client advice, which may not always be what they want to hear, or to negotiate with HMRC when arguing your client's case. These skills are very similar to those of a lawyer and law graduates are much in demand to train as tax accountants (although graduates in any subject, and also non-graduates, can specialise in tax).

> Peter the Great, Tsar of Russia from 1682 to 1725, was so keen to find new ways to tax his subjects that he set up a committee of 'fiscals' to help him. Taxes on boots, beehives, beards, hats, horses, candles, chimneys, melons, cucumbers and even drinking water were just some of the ideas they came up with.

Tax work offers constant change and variety: tax law never stands still, so you need to keep your knowledge up to date. This is particularly important when the government presents its Budget: you will need to absorb a large amount of new information in a short time, understand how this could affect your clients and pass the information on to them along with recommendations for any action they may need to take. It also demands the ability to come up with innovative ideas and creative solutions to your clients' problems.

The regular cycle of the tax year means that, although there are extremely busy times, these can normally be foreseen and planned for well ahead. Budget day and the deadline for filing personal tax returns are when tax work peaks: otherwise the working hours are normally more regular, and the work–life balance more even, than in other areas of accountancy.

If you are certain that tax is for you, you can specialise in it from the very beginning of your career by studying for the exams of the Association of Taxation Technicians. This is a qualification in its own right which can also be used as a route to membership of the Chartered Institute of Taxation (CIOT). You could alternatively train as a chartered or certified accountant, gaining experience in tax during your training contract and then top up this qualification by taking the CIOT's Chartered Tax Adviser qualification. HMRC also recruits trainee accountants, who can choose between the ICAEW, CIMA and ACCA qualifications.

Insolvency

When the economic climate gets tough, the insolvency specialists get going. The failures of big-name companies, such as Woolworths, Zavvi and Waterford Wedgwood, make headlines, but the recession has caused many less high-profile casualties, with the Insolvency Service recording almost 12,000 businesses going into liquidation in the first half of 2009.

A company is said to be insolvent when it has insufficient resources to pay the money it owes to its creditors. In this situation it may go into administration, which gives it breathing space to try and work out a solution. When a company is in administration, the assets that it still possesses, such as stock or buildings, are protected from being seized by its creditors while the administrator works with the management team to try and save the company.

Saving the company is usually the preferred option and insolvency does not have to be a death sentence. For this reason, many accounting firms have rebranded their insolvency practices with more upbeat and positive names, such as 'business recovery' or 'restructuring'.

Insolvency practitioners who are appointed as administrators will often take over responsibility for the management of the business and keep it running while a rescue plan is being worked out. They will analyse the business and its problems, looking at issues such as cashflow, business strategies and raising capital; they will negotiate with creditors; and they may be able to return the business to its owners in a better state of financial health. At the same time, they will be actively involved in the day-to-day running of the business, taking management decisions, liaising and negotiating with customers, suppliers and employees.

This is not always possible, in which case the next option is for the administrators to try and find a buyer for the company, as a whole or in part. If all else fails and the company cannot be restructured or sold, the administrators will liquidate it, dispose of its assets and repay its creditors from the proceeds according to the procedures established by law.

This can involve a great deal of investigative work to establish exactly what the assets are and how they can be recovered.

Insolvency work can be very hands-on and practical. As well as dealing with the company's owners and directors, insolvency practitioners must work with impatient creditors, anxious employees, bankers, lawyers, the Insolvency Service and, in high-profile cases, the media. To do this demands confidence, diplomacy, sensitivity and very good communication skills. It also demands being able to get to grips quickly with all areas of the business and the problems it is facing, using initiative and working under pressure.

Insolvency practitioners work in accountancy firms or in specialist firms of licensed insolvency practitioners. They come from different backgrounds and not all are accountants. An accountancy qualification is, however, highly relevant and gives a strong understanding of the variety of clients, businesses and problems that you are likely to come across in this varied, unpredictable and demanding area.

Max works in Pricewaterhouse-Coopers LLP's Business Recovery Services (BRS) department in London.

'Accountancy seemed to me to be a way of gaining an introduction into the world of business, whilst also obtaining an internationally recognised qualification. Once I'd made the decision to go into accountancy, I wanted to try and gain my ACA qualification in the most interesting way possible and felt that the hands-on commercial experience offered within Business Recovery Services would do this for me.

'BRS is very much project-based, and what you are doing on a day-to-day basis depends entirely on what kind of project you are working on. You could be on an industrial estate in Croydon helping to keep a company in administration trading, or you could be in the office writing an independent business review (which aims to clarify the current financial and/or operational status of a business and the range of options available in the short and longer term) or employer covenant review (an objective and independent assessment of the overall financial strength of participating employers of a pension scheme). Currently I am working on a restructuring, which at the moment involves a lot of detailed modelling of a company's projections, with the aim of resetting the covenants on their debt going forward.

'Anyone hoping to go into accountancy should work hard and try and get as much work experience as you can. In addition, the more you can read the financial press, and improve your knowledge of how things work in the world of business, the better.'

Only the largest accountancy firms, or niche insolvency practices, are likely to give you the chance of specialising in this area during your training. Those that do will normally require you to qualify as a chartered or certified accountant, which will involve spending time in audit work in order to meet these institutes' requirements for professional training. Even if you don't specialise in insolvency as a trainee, there are plenty of opportunities to move into this field after you qualify and to enhance your accountancy qualifications by taking the exams of the Joint Insolvency Examinations Board (JIEB) and becoming a licensed Insolvency Practitioner (IP).

Forensic accounting

Forensic accountants don't wear white lab coats and are unlikely to be found at crime scenes. While forensic accountancy does involve investigation and detective work it isn't just about fraud and crime – although the accounting scandals described in Chapter 2 have certainly contributed to the growth in this area. Forensic accountancy investigations also cover divorce settlements, personal injury and insurance claims and a whole range of disputes, such as the example below from Quantis Forensic Accountants.

A pie maker was forced to move out of his premises when the local authority issued a Compulsory Purchase Order. Forensic accountants helped him to put together a compensation claim for the cost of relocation and the disturbance that would be caused to the business, which normally produced 4,000 meat pies a day.

The local authority then obtained its own expert accountancy report, putting a much lower value on the claim. The pie maker's accountants were able to show that the other experts had not fully appreciated how the business operated and the company was able to obtain full compensation.

'Investigation' is the key word: forensic accountants study accounts, other documents and computer records, looking for evidence to support their client's case. They also gather evidence through talking to people, both at formal interviews and more informally, and work closely with other experts such as lawyers, insurance assessors, the police and regulatory bodies.

Forensic accounting demands skills similar to those needed in auditing, and many forensic accountants begin their careers as external auditors. One key difference is that auditors are hoping that everything in their client's affairs is open and above board, while forensic accountants are looking for evidence of wrongdoing, so they need to be more wary of taking things at face value. Curiosity, a good eye for detail and the ability to spot anything unusual are essential. You will spend a good deal of your time working with people who may not have much understanding of accountancy, so you will need to be able to explain things to them in a clear and concise way, in writing or orally – this could include acting as an expert witness in court.

Many large firms have a forensic accounting department and it may be possible to gain some experience in this area during chartered or certified accountancy training. A few specialist forensic accounting firms do train chartered or certified accountants, but it is more usual to move into this area after qualification. As yet, there is no specialist qualification in forensic accounting and forensic accountants' expertise is built up by on-the-job training and experience. Besides firms, there are also opportunities in government bodies such as the Serious Fraud Office, the Serious Organised Crime Agency (SOCA), the Securities and Investment Institute and HMRC.

Public sector

All of the roles and activities covered in this chapter can be part of the work of accountants in the public sector as well as the private sector. However, as there are some distinctive aspects of finance work in public bodies and other not-for-profit organisations, this sector has been included as an area of work in its own right.

The public sector in the UK spends almost £700 billion pounds every year on public services such as defence, law and order, education and training, health, social services and transport. Almost a fifth of the working population are employed in central and local government, the NHS (the largest employer in Europe) and other public bodies. Public spending often makes headlines, and the way 'taxpayers' money' is used by public bodies is under constant scrutiny. Accountants are essential to ensure that public money is used effectively and that information is available to stakeholders. They also play a key role in providing the information used by public sector managers to decide how public money should be used – and, at senior levels, in helping to take those decisions.

The day-to-day work of accountants in the public sector is similar in many ways to that of their counterparts in the private sector. Like other organisations, public sector bodies need to use financial data to prepare and produce accounts, budgets and forecasts and to provide information for management and stakeholders. The most significant differences in the work of in-house accountants in the public and private sectors lie in the issues that their work is concerned with and the regulatory environment.

Budgeting in the public sector involves allocating what is usually a limited amount of financial resources across a number of services. Some of these services, such as healthcare, education and social services, are very high profile and affect the everyday lives of thousands, or even millions, of people. While high-level decisions on the allocation of public funds will be taken by elected representatives, they rely on senior public sector finance managers to advise them on financial issues and possible outcomes before making these decisions.

Regulation and control are of even greater importance in the public sector than the private sector, given the vast sums of taxpayers' money involved and the commitment of public bodies to 'transparency' – making information about the way they operate freely available and clearly understandable. A large proportion of the work of accountants in the public sector is therefore spent in ensuring that compliance and control systems are functioning effectively. Internal audits are also used extensively for this purpose.

Value for money (VFM) audits, ensuring that public bodies are delivering services economically, efficiently and effectively, are another feature of the public sector. These cover a wide range of issues, not all of which are specifically financial, but accountants are normally involved in planning and conducting the audit.

Financial information collected from local authorities and health services may be used at top levels of government to provide government ministers with material for taking policy decisions, answering questions in Parliament and determining public spending at national level. The impact of accountants' work can therefore go far beyond their direct employer.

Not all of these accountants are employed in the public sector itself – an increasing number of accountancy firms provide both external and internal audit services to public sector clients.

Although CIPFA qualifications are specifically tailored for the public sector, any professional accountancy or accounting technician qualification is also relevant and can be used in this sector.

Charities

Charities are not technically part of the public sector – they are independent organisations – but accountants working in charities face many of the same issues as those in the public sector. Charities often work closely with government bodies, such as social services departments and the National Lottery and, like public sector bodies, operate within a tightly controlled system that regulates and monitors their spending and the way they operate. A large proportion of the work of charity accountants involves preparing detailed bids for funding and then ensuring through financial reporting that funds donated in this way are used as stipulated by the donor. Accountants in charities also work with tax issues that are specific to charities, such as gift aid and payroll giving, and with aspects of charities' activities that are treated as commercial ventures, such as shops and online retailing. Any of the professional qualifications can be used in the charity sector, but only the largest charities are likely to employ their own accountants. There are therefore a number of accountants in private practice firms who specialise in working with charity clients.

Central government departments, local authorities, the NHS, the National Audit Office and the Financial Services Authority all employ large numbers of accountants and recruit graduates to train for professional accountancy qualifications. Charities and other not-for-profit organisations employ qualified accountants but are less likely to offer professional training. Accountancy firms in private practice often work extensively with public sector bodies and it is possible to train with some of these firms for the CIPFA qualification.

William is a principal accountant with Surrey County Council.

'To be honest, accountancy was not a career path I had planned to go into. I did a degree in history and my plan was to work internationally in the not-for-profit sector, probably doing some form of project management. I was actually learning Russian and teaching English as a foreign language when I came across a job advert for a graduate trainee scheme called Accountants for the Future (ATF). This was run jointly by the Metropolitan Police Service and the

London Boroughs of Hackney and Islington and involved six-month rotating placements across the three organisations over a three-year period, during which time we were supported to study for the CIPFA qualification.

'CIPFA is the premier qualification for people working in finance in the public sector. The nature of this sector means that students have to learn and apply financial techniques to a wide range of different scenarios and situations and, in studying CIPFA, you are taught to use your common sense but at the same time always be aware of the fundamental principles of accounting. The management theory and softer people skills CIPFA trainees are taught and develop also mean that they are able to adapt and fit in with different cultures: this made the transition between placements reasonably straightforward, even though there were quite significant differences in their working cultures, most notably when moving between the police and the councils.

'The ATF scheme came to an end when I qualified in August 2007, but this qualification, and the experience I had gained on the scheme, opened up a number of job opportunities. I was successful in gaining a full-time position at Islington Council, as management accountant in the Environment and Regeneration finance team, where I worked for almost two and half years.

'Whilst working in E&R I supported the Strategic Planning and Regeneration and Environmental Sustainability divisions. My core role was to ensure accurate budgets were set for these divisions and to monitor actual spend against these budgets throughout the year. This was not just a back-office accountancy function: my work in monitoring actuals against budgets was vital in helping service managers to effectively manage their budgets and ensure that value for money was delivered to the local community. I advised senior managers and service directors about where to target resources most effectively and also helped to offer potential solutions to budget problems that arose.

'In January 2010 I left my role in Islington to take up a principal accountant position in Surrey County Council's Adult Social Care finance team. Almost immediately, I became heavily involved in work to finalise the directorate's medium-term financial plan and also in negotiations with local Primary Care Trusts regarding funding for the transfer of learning disability clients to the council's social care framework. I had to get to grips quickly with new, complex information, and my CIPFA studies combined with my experience in public sector finance helped me to do this.

'Over the next few years the public sector will face a number of challenges, in particular:

- the ongoing financial downturn and the knock-on effect this is having on public sector funding. Public bodies will have to struggle to continue to improve their service provision with fewer resources. An added pressure is that demand for services is likely to increase as unemployment goes up

- the pressures, both financial and logistical, of an ageing population, with more elderly people seeking public sector support and conversely fewer people of working age to provide those services

- the increasing impact of climate change on all public bodies as they have to find innovative ways to meet the government's emissions targets.

'I think CPFAs are well equipped to face all of these challenges as they have the right mix of financial and non-financial skills to enable them to adapt and innovate according to the varying circumstances faced by public sector organisations.

'On a personal note, I hope to move into more senior strategic positions in the future and, whether I remain in a purely financial role or branch out into strategic or project management, I feel I will be well placed to make these transitions as a result of my CIPFA qualification and the opportunities it has afforded me. My work has a direct impact on how effectively services are delivered to the local community: for me, this is much more satisfying than seeking to maximise company profits in the private sector would be.'

Chapter Four
TRAINING, SKILLS AND QUALIFICATIONS

WHAT QUALIFICATIONS DO YOU NEED TO WORK AS AN ACCOUNTANT?

Legally, anyone can call themselves an accountant even if they have no formal qualifications at all! Unlike, for example, 'dentist' or 'architect', this is not a legally defined professional title in the UK.

This does not mean, though, that the accountancy profession is completely unregulated – quite the opposite. There are a number of professional bodies that control the training and qualification of accountants and regulate their day-to-day work, ensuring that professional standards are maintained.

In addition, certain types of accounting work (such as audit and insolvency work) can legally only be carried out by people with a recognised qualification.

This means that employers and clients can be sure that an accountant who has qualified with one of these bodies has achieved a high standard of knowledge and practical skills and is able to carry out their work effectively and to professional standards.

Qualifying as an accountant involves both passing a number of exams and gaining approved experience working in accountancy. Many trainee accountants study part time for their exams while working for an employer under a 'training contract', which provides them with support (such as study leave and tuition fees) for their professional training.

Professional bodies

To recap Chapter 1, there are six professional bodies which offer chartered accountancy qualifications: four of these are generalist and two more specialised. The four general bodies are:

1   **ICAEW:** Institute of Chartered Accountants in England and Wales

2   **ICAS:** Institute of Chartered Accountants of Scotland

3   **ICAI:** Chartered Accountants Ireland (Institute of Chartered Accountants in Ireland)

4   **ACCA:** Association of Chartered Certified Accountants.

These four institutes offer a broad-based qualification which, once you are qualified, will allow you to work in practically any area of accountancy, including work as an auditor and/or an insolvency practitioner. The vast majority of students in the three institutes of chartered accountants, though, train in accountancy firms in private practice. ACCA trainees may train in firms but also train in industry, commerce and the public sector.

The qualifications offered by the other two institutes provide somewhat less breadth but greater depth and therefore allow you to specialise from the beginning of your training.

1   **CIMA:** (Chartered Institute of Management Accountants) focuses on the education and training of management accountants in industry, commerce and the public and not-for-profit sectors.

2   **CIPFA:** (Chartered Institute of Public Finance and Accountancy) specialises in public services. Most chartered public finance accountants work in central and local government, the NHS and other public bodies, but some work in private practice firms.

The six chartered accountancy bodies are all members of the Consultative Committee of Accountancy Bodies (CCAB), through which they co-operate to represent the accountancy profession as a whole. CCAB does not award qualifications itself, but some job advertisements use the term 'CCAB qualified' to mean any one of the above six qualifications. This generally means that the employer requires an accountant who is qualified at chartered level, but is relaxed about which institute has awarded that qualification.

Table 4 Where do students train?

	ACCA	CIMA	CIPFA	ICAEW	ICAI	ICAS	Total
Private practice	73,329 (24%)	0	0	12,058 (75%)	5,655 (95%)	3,343 (96.5%)	94,385
Industry & commerce	153,994 (50%)	71,798 (78%)	67 (2%)	241 (1.5%)	183 (3%)	123 (3.5%)	226,406
Public sector	40,433 (13%)	16,451 (18%)	2,759 (96%)	217 (1.5%)	12 (0.2%)	0	59,872
Others	39,701 (13%)	3,275 (4%)	59 (2%)	3,649 (22%)	108 (1.8%)	0	46,792
Total	307,457	91,524	2,885	16,165	5,958	3,466	427,455

WHAT OTHER QUALIFICATIONS ARE AVAILABLE?

Other recognised bodies that provide professional training in accountancy and related areas include the AAT, CIOT/ATT and AIA.

AAT

The Association of Accounting Technicians (AAT) offers qualifications in a number of areas, including accounting, payroll administration and bookkeeping. These qualifications are widely recognised in their own right, but will also give you exemptions from the chartered accountancy bodies' exams.

CIOT/ATT

The Chartered Institute of Taxation and its sister body, the Association of Taxation Technicians, provide specialised training and qualifications in tax work. These can be taken independently or as a follow-up to one of the accountancy qualifications.

AIA

The Association of International Accountants offers a professional qualification recognised in over 30 countries worldwide. It is a recognised qualifying body for auditors in the UK and across the European Union. The exam syllabus aims to balance global business and local knowledge.

When you qualify, you will be able to use the following letters after your name.

Table 5 Qualifications and titles

Awarding institute	Title
ICAEW and ICAI	ACA (Associate Chartered Accountant)
ICAS	CA (Chartered Accountant)
ACCA	ACCA (Associate Chartered Certified Accountant)
AAT	MAAT (Member of the Association of Accounting Technicians)
CIMA	ACMA (Associate Chartered Management Accountant)
CIPFA	CPFA (Chartered Public Finance Accountant)
AIA	AAIA (Associate of the Association of International Accountants)

As the world's oldest professional accountancy body, and the first to use the term 'chartered accountant', ICAS is the only one of the chartered accountancy institutes to use the initials 'CA' on their own to designate members.

CHOOSING YOUR QUALIFICATION

With so many different professional bodies, choosing the right qualification can seem difficult. However, there is quite a lot of overlap between the training and exams offered by the different institutes. Some of the points you may want to consider include the following.

What type of organisation do you want to work for?

If you know exactly what type of accountancy, or type of business, you want to work in, some qualifications may be more appropriate than others. If you don't have a clear idea at this stage, don't worry – many accountancy qualifications can be used across a wide range of employers and job roles.

The most flexible qualifications are those offered by the chartered and certified accountancy institutes. While the majority of ICAEW, ICAS and ICAI students train in private practice, only about 30% of qualified members overall actually work in this sector while over 40% work in industry, commerce or the public sector. ACCA-qualified accountants can also work in all these areas, and move between them even while they are still students.

Because of their greater specialisation, the CIMA and CIPFA qualifications are not quite as transferable between different sectors so, if you choose to study for one of these, you need to be quite certain that this is where you want your career to be. If you are already sure that industry and commerce, or the public sector, is for you, then you can focus on it from the start of your training. If you want to work in these areas but still keep your options open, some employers give their trainees a choice of professional qualification – often this choice is between ACCA and CIMA, but you may be able to train with one of the other institutes.

Where do you want to train?

Geographical location may influence your choice of qualification, although not always as much as you might think. Accountants are found everywhere, and so are organisations that employ and train them. Where the body that oversees your training is located does not always matter: ICAS, for example, actually has more training centres in England than it does in Scotland, and it also has centres in Jersey and Luxembourg. ICAEW qualification programmes are available in China, Cyprus, Greece, the Gulf, India, Malaysia, Pakistan, Romania, Russia and Singapore. You can study for CIMA qualifications in 30 countries around the world, while the ACCA qualification is available in 170 countries.

How will you study and what exams will you take?

Something else to look at when you are making your choice is the structure of the training and of the exams that you will need to take. When you are comparing the training provided by the different Institutes, you may want to consider issues such as these.

- How many exams will I need to take?

- Do I need to take a number of exams at each sitting or could I just take one or two papers at a time?

- What exemptions might I get for my previous qualifications or experience?

- Where can I study for the exams?

- What is the pass rate for the exams?

- Will my study be organised in intensive blocks of full-time study or will it be spread out part time over a longer period?

Will your qualification be recognised in other countries?

All the professional accountancy qualifications carry international recognition. ACCA is the most international qualification, but CIMA has over 15,000 members working outside the British Isles and the ICAEW almost 20,000. The smaller size of the Irish and Scottish institutes is no barrier to an international career, with around 10% of their members working overseas.

The CIPFA qualification does not travel so well, as public sectors in different countries vary so widely and the CIPFA qualification is designed specifically for those working in the public sector in the UK. This doesn't mean that CIPFA-qualified accountants are restricted to the UK, though – a small percentage of them do work abroad and the qualification is recognised internationally.

Choosing an accountancy qualification is rather like choosing a degree course and university – what is right for one individual will not suit another. Researching the different institutes, and the employers who might support your training for their qualifications, is essential.

WHAT QUALIFICATIONS DO I NEED TO START TRAINING AS AN ACCOUNTANT?

Although accountancy is one of the most popular career choices for graduates, it is possible to start training as an accountant even without formal qualifications: from school or college or as a career changer.

From school or college

A number of chartered accountancy firms offer training contracts to candidates with A levels or equivalent qualifications. You will need good grades in these exams – at least 220 UCAS points, although many employers will ask for 280. These A levels can be in any subject – you don't have to have A level maths. You should, though, have a good GCSE grade in maths and also in English. Training contracts for school and college leavers are usually longer than those offered to graduates and may last four, or even five, years.

Table 6 on the next page shows the number of UCAS points allocated to different qualifications and gives an indication of how the points awarded for individual papers might add up to the points totals that firms may ask for. (The totals for three or more exams may have been rounded up or down on the chart.) You should in any case check the current position on the UCAS website (www.ucas.com), which also shows the points for other qualifications not covered here.

Most non-graduate entrants to the accountancy profession will train initially for an accounting technician qualification such as the AAT Accounting Qualification. You don't need any formal qualifications to enrol as a student with AAT but if you do have GCSEs, A levels or equivalent qualifications you will be able to start your training at a higher level. Not all employers specify a minimum UCAS points score for candidates with A levels or equivalent, but some may ask for 260 points or more. The AAT qualification will take between two and three years to complete and covers a mixture of theoretical knowledge and practical accounting skills.

Qualified accounting technicians can then go on to qualify with one of the chartered accountancy bodies: all these accept the AAT as an entry qualification and it will give you exemption from some of their exams.

Table 6 How to work out your UCAS points

UCAS points	A level	Advanced Higher	Higher	IB Diploma
320	ABB		AAAA	27
300	BBB	BBC	AAAB	26
280	BBC	BCC	AABB	25
260	BCC	BCD	BBBC	24
220	CCD	CDD	BBCD	
140	A*			
130		A	BB	
120	A			
110		B		
100	B			
90		C		
80	C		A	
72		D		
65			B	
60	D			
50			C	
40	E			
36			D	

David is an ACCA trainee at Ensors, a large regional firm in East Anglia.

'I have always wanted a creditable profession and wanted to be a lawyer or an accountant. At the age of 15 I had a two-week work experience placement in the accounts department of a nuclear power station and from there I decided on a career in accountancy. I kept my options open by applying to university but was offered an AAT training position with Ensors and, having passed my A levels with the required grades, started work with the firm in August 2006.

'The AAT qualification is a great stepping stone to a career in accountancy, but starting off with no previous knowledge straight from A levels is difficult. Like many other people, at first I didn't understand a lot of the tasks and jobs I was carrying out. Before long, though, through my study and training, things started to click into place and I started to understand the meanings and principles behind the tasks that I was completing. One of the best moments in my career so far was when I became AAT qualified after two years of training.

'I am currently a year and a half into my ACCA qualification, which I chose due to its worldwide recognition, and have completed seven out of my 14 exams. If all goes well I will be qualified by August 2011 so I will become qualified more quickly than I would have done if I had chosen to go to university before starting my accountancy training.

'My exam study is on a block release basis: we normally get nine days' study leave per exam and sit four exams a year so I'm studying for 36 of the 260 working days a year – plus revision in my own time before the exams. The exam sittings are in December and June every year: it's not very nice having exams so near Christmas but, as they normally take place in the first week in December, it still gives time to look forward and plan for Christmas.

'At the moment, I am in the business services department, where most of my work is office based, although I do occasionally attend stocktakes and go out on audit. Probably my most unusual experience was attending a stocktake for a large poultry factory and seeing the whole of the poultry cycle, from being fed and fattened to being culled and packaged for shops. If I were in the company audit department I would spend much more time on audit, but as it is I go on about four audits a year, which last about three days per audit on average.

'I normally get into the office at 8.45 a.m. and common tasks involve work on completing and producing accounts (working out clients' profit or loss in a year) and completing the tax returns that follow from this. I work with all sorts of clients, mostly clients with their own businesses such as sole traders, partnerships, trusts and limited companies. You get an insight into the business environment and see many different trades and professions.

'I haven't been pigeonholed into one area but have gained experience of all sorts of aspects of accountancy, interacted with clients and developed my people skills, all of which gives me a good foundation for the future. Within the next five years I would like to see myself achieve ACCA membership and then gain a client list of my own and head towards progressing my career in accountancy.

'I know now I made the right choice by not going to university and have gained many benefits from training through the AAT route. I will become qualified as a chartered certified accountant without any of the debts that I would have accumulated by going to university. My firm pays me a salary, pays for all the training materials, study courses and exam fees – and I didn't need to take out any student loans!'

From university

Every year, approximately 10% of all graduates in the UK begin training with one of the professional accountancy bodies. These graduates come from a wide range of degree backgrounds.

The ICAEW, ICAS and ICAI have the highest percentage of graduate entrants, but the differences in the educational qualifications of those entering the various training schemes are often a result of the selection policies adopted by employers rather than the accountancy bodies themselves.

Your degree can be in any subject and does not have to be relevant to accounting, finance or business. As the bar chart below shows, 'non-relevant' graduate trainees outnumber 'relevant' graduates in all the professional bodies except the ICAI.

Percentage of students holding a degree and percentage of those students holding a relevant degree (2008)

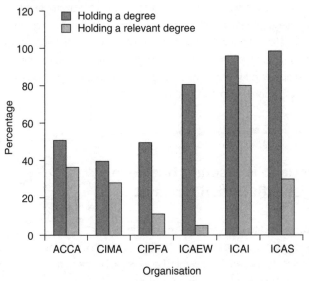

It is difficult to draw conclusions from the percentage of students holding 'relevant degrees' as the accountancy bodies use different definitions of a relevant degree. Some count all business-related subjects as relevant, while others only count accounting degrees. The broad definitions of a relevant degree used by the different bodies are as follows:

■ **ACCA:** accountancy, business

■ **CIMA:** accountancy, business studies, business administration, finance, accountancy

- **CIPFA:** accountancy

- **ICAEW:** accountancy, accounting and finance, finance

- **ICAI:** accountancy, business and commerce, finance

- **ICAS:** accountancy.

If you do have a relevant degree, all the institutes will give you some exemptions from the professional exams. Most accounting degrees cover the same ground as the first-stage professional exams and include financial accounting, management accounting, financial reporting, business and management and business law. A degree in accounting could therefore exempt you from the whole of the first stage, providing that you have chosen appropriate modules. If you have a degree in business, economics, law or a related subject, you will get exemptions from the first-stage papers in these subject areas. Since the requirements of the various institutes not only differ from one another, but are subject to change from time to time, you should check the position on exemptions when you are applying for university and again when you start to apply for graduate training schemes in accountancy.

Amandeep is a senior business analyst with British Airways.

'I've always liked to know where I'm going and I started to plan my career around the time I was choosing my GCSE subjects. I knew that I wanted a career in business and that accountancy would be a good way into this, but I was also interested in the bigger picture so I was pleased to find out that I didn't have to do an accountancy degree to become an accountant! I studied economics at both A level and university and then took a master's degree in finance, economics and econometrics. Whilst studying for this, I registered with some recruitment agencies and, when I graduated, began my ACCA training on a finance graduate scheme with a car rental company.

'The recruitment agencies kept my details on file, and after a few months I was approached with an opportunity at British Midland Airways (BMI) that was just too good to miss. I joined BMI as a business accountant for Airport and Cabin Services. I looked after all the European stations and worldwide lounges, creating and managing the budget for each area. I was involved in negotiating contracts, tender offers, looking at ways to cut costs and implementing new business processes, building relationships with non-finance managers and regularly presenting to senior management. It was a fantastic experience, but after two years I decided it was time to look for a new role. Although I hadn't specifically planned to stay in the airline industry, and had job offers from several other employers, I chose British Airways (BA) because of the company's reputation, its platinum status with the ACCA, and the positive feedback I got from people working there.

'I joined BA as a financial analyst for aircraft modifications in the engineering finance division. I looked after the business, financial and monthly forecast plans for all aircraft modifications, whilst carrying out management and financial accounting for the area. This role allowed me to get involved in the more technical aspects of accounting, and I was exposed to a variety of projects, balance sheets, internal and external audit, as well as developing a profitability model and taking on accountable finance manager responsibility.

'I'm now a senior business analyst for the Europe, Asia Pacific and Africa region, working as part of a team of analysts covering all the commercial, customer service and strategic transformation functions within this region. It's a really varied role and stretches well beyond the parameters of finance. The exposure to the overseas finance teams allows for a better understanding of different business models, local legislation and cultural awareness as well as providing a broader view of

BA's global operations. I'm involved in projects looking at all kinds of business issues, from building new process models, to the impact of the economic climate on our performance. As well as this project work, there are the regular month-end tasks where we analyse the monthly accounts so that we can keep departments informed about what has been happening recently in financial terms and what action they need to take. Our team works with commercial managers to support them in planning their budgets, reducing their costs and increasing revenue, so it is important to be commercially and economically aware. It's all about building relationships, talking to people, getting to understand the business as a whole and being able to ask the right questions.

'Fitting in study alongside the day-to-day work can be difficult, but getting the right balance is crucial. The ACCA qualification has always been important to me and one of my reasons for choosing the different employers I've worked with was the study support that they would provide. I chose the ACCA because the qualification provides good technical accounting training and allows you to work in all areas of accountancy and finance, including audit and tax, so I could keep my options open. The opportunity to get a further degree (a BSc in Applied Accounting from Oxford Brookes University) alongside the professional qualification was another attraction. I have just one more paper to take now and, once I pass that, will be fully qualified as I have already completed the required three years of practical work experience.

'Completing the qualification will be a great achievement: I'll be proud to say I'm ACCA qualified and look forward to progressing my career with British Airways by taking up more challenging opportunities and continuing with my professional development. The finance function is not just about accountancy – it's whatever you want to make of it.'

It doesn't matter how many, or how few, exemptions you have: it will still take you three years to qualify. Graduates with relevant degrees may get through all their exams before those with non-relevant degrees, but three years' approved work experience is still essential before you become qualified.

Some employers require all their trainees, whatever their degree background, to attend the study courses for the first-stage exams. Relevant graduates will not actually need to take the exams at the end of the course, but employers find that it is useful for them to refresh their knowledge of subjects that they may have taken a few years before starting their training and to study them from a practical, rather than an academic, point of view.

Graduates are normally expected to have achieved a minimum 2.2 degree, but many employers will look for a 2.1. A postgraduate degree, even in business or finance, is not normally required or seen as offering any substantial advantage: the professional exams are challenging enough in themselves and are focused on professional practice, so most employers will prefer students to get started on these as soon as possible.

Good grades from school or college are still important, even if you also have a degree. Many employers see these grades as a better indication of your ability to pass the professional exams than your degree class, as the study methods and exams have more similarities than those at university. Employers therefore often require between 280 and 300 UCAS points.

As a mature entrant/career changer

The AAT qualification outlined above is open to all entrants, regardless of previous qualifications or experience, and is therefore popular with non-graduate mature entrants and career changers. If you do have previous experience relevant to accountancy or finance, you may be able to start your training at a higher level; if you are currently working in a finance-related role, this can be used in your training and assessment.

Some of the professional institutes offer their own qualifications at an equivalent level. These include the ACCA's Certified Accounting Technician (CAT) qualification and the CIMA Certificate in Business Accounting. Like the AAT qualification, they do not require previous experience or qualifications and can be used as a 'stepping stone' to the full professional qualification.

The Open University Professional Certificate in Accounting is a new course covering financial and management accounting and the role of accounting in business organisations. Although the course has not yet been recognised by the professional bodies, the OU expects it to be accredited by ACCA and CIMA, allowing holders of the certificate to progress to professional training in accounting. The Open University website (www.open.ac.uk), or the institutes' websites, will give you further details.

Graduates whose degree class and/or A level grades are below the standard that employers normally ask for, but who have gained experience since graduation which helps them to demonstrate business awareness or relevant personal skills, may find that this will compensate for their earlier results and help them to be accepted on to graduate training schemes. Alternatively, you could study independently for some of the first-level papers of the professional exams and apply for trainee positions once you have demonstrated that you are capable of passing these exams.

WHAT DOES QUALIFYING INVOLVE?

Exams

Whichever institute you train with, you will need to pass a number of tough exams in order to qualify – professional accountancy qualifications are generally considered to be at least at the same level as an undergraduate degree.

The exams are structured in two or three stages, depending on which institute sets them. You will normally need to pass all the exams at one level before you can proceed to the next level. The exams themselves may be online or paper based, traditional or multiple choice, depending on the institute setting them and the level of the exam.

At the first level, you will study both financial accounting and management accounting, along with other topics such as business law, tax and professional ethics. You will learn key practical skills, such as how to prepare accounts and use double-entry accounting techniques.

Once you have completed this level (the time it takes will depend on the institute, any exemptions you have and whether you are studying full time or part time), you will continue to develop your financial accounting and management accounting skills and knowledge and to relate them to the workplace and to the wider business and finance environment.

Table 7 An outline of the exam structure for the professional qualifications of the chartered accountancy institutes

Institute	First stage	Second stage	Third stage
ACCA	Fundamentals (9 papers)	Professional (5 papers)	…
CIMA	Managerial Level (8 papers) Management Level (93 papers)	Strategic Level (3 papers)	Test of Professional Competence
CIPFA	Certificate (4 papers)	Diploma (7 papers)	Test of Professional Competence
ICAEW	Professional Stage (6 knowledge modules, 6 application modules)	Advanced Stage (3 modules)	…
ICAI	CA Proficiency 1 (5 papers)	CA Proficiency 2 (4 papers)	Final Admitting Examination (FAE)
ICAS	Test of Competence (5 papers)	Test of Professional Skills (4 subjects)	Test of Professional Expertise

The final level in all institutes includes a case study which tests your ability to apply the professional skills and knowledge gained through the earlier stages to a realistic business scenario.

> The final case study exam is very different from the papers at the earlier stages. It tests your practical abilities rather than your academic knowledge and is like doing the job in real life. You can bring in situations that you have come across during your training and base the advice you give to the fictional case study client on these. It's a challenging exam and you need to be able to give good practical advice.
>
> ICAS-qualified accountant

Studying for the exams

You can study for the professional exams in a variety of ways: full time or part time; face-to-face tuition or online learning

Most employers of accounting students will send their trainees to one of the tutorial firms that specialise in providing training for the various professional exams. The courses they offer can be taken in evening classes, in full-time courses (which may last as little as one week or as long as three months), or by day release. You can also enrol on these courses as an independent student. The Scottish and Irish institutes run their own training courses.

Training for the professional accountancy qualifications in larger organisations is usually highly structured and will typically involve in-house training as well as attending professional courses. In-house training may complement the external courses or may be linked to the firm's procedures and practices or be used to prepare you for a new area of work.

Employers of trainee accountants will cover the costs involved in these courses and the terms of your contract will provide you with time off work to attend them.

The amount of time that you will have to spend studying depends to a considerable extent on you, your employer and the professional qualification you are taking. Many employers will include study time in your working hours but you shouldn't underestimate the time that you will need to devote to studying on top of your work. In large accountancy firms, about 20% of your working time could be allocated to study: in smaller firms, you will probably have slightly less of your time set aside for study and will have to do more studying outside working hours. In general, between 12 and 15 hours a week of study is recommended to keep up with the workload.

> *You do get study leave, but you need to put more time than this into study if you want to do well in the exams. It does eat into your social life, which is annoying when all your friends are going out having a good time.*
>
> *Trainee in a medium-sized London firm*

Work experience

Passing the exams on their own does not make you a qualified accountant. You will also need to complete a period of approved work experience (usually three years) with an employer that is authorised by the relevant institute to train you. While you can begin your training, and take some of the exams, before you start working in accountancy, the final stage of the exams can usually only be taken after you have gained some relevant experience: this is because the exams are not simply theoretical but are designed to show how you can apply what you have learned in your day-to-day work.

Katie is a second-year trainee at PKF, one of the top 10 accountancy firms.

case
STUDY

Katie chose an accountancy career as a route into the public sector but is doing her training in private practice, which gives her the chance to gain a broad range of experience of different types of client while still being able to focus on the public sector. She chose this route following a summer internship with her present employer, which has a large number of clients in the public sector.

All graduate trainees at PKF, whichever part of the UK they are based in, take the ICAS qualification. The study for this qualification is organised on an intensive, block-release basis which involves eight weeks of full-time study in the first year and 12 weeks in the second year, meaning that work and study are completely separated. Each block of study is immediately followed by a set of exams, which means that, after less than 18 months with the firm, Katie has now completed all her professional exams apart from the final stage – a big case study which she will take in November of her third year.

PKF has a wide range of clients, from small charities to large public companies and local authorities, offering a variety of work. Katie is training in audit and therefore spends over 80% of her time out of the office, working at clients' premises. The time that she does spend in the office is taken up with planning and preparing for audits, which vary in length from a couple of days to six weeks. The largest clients are generally the most complex, especially large PLCs with a number of subsidiaries which all need to be audited separately before being brought together to complete the audit as a whole.

From the end of her second year, Katie will be able to specialise in working with the public sector clients that are her main interest. She particularly enjoys working with central government departments and looking at issues of particular concern to the public sector, such as value for money. Once she qualifies, there will be a number of opportunities open to her in central or local government, the NHS or in consultancy work but, whichever she chooses, she feels that her training in practice and her ICAS qualification will be a good preparation.

How much will it cost to qualify?

It may not cost you anything in money terms. Many accountancy firms and industrial, commercial and public sector employers will not only pay their trainee accountants a salary while they are training but will also cover the costs of their exam tuition and study materials and the fees for sitting exams. They are also likely to give you paid study leave to prepare for your exams.

Details of what your employer will offer you will be set out in your training contract or contract of employment, along with any terms and conditions. For example, there may be a clause which says that your employer will only pay for your first attempt at any exam and that if you need to resit any paper you will need to pay the exam fee yourself. These fees range from £50 to £250 per paper.

If you do have to pay your own tuition fees, these will vary according to how and where you study, but typically range from about £200 to £600 per paper. You do not have to enrol with a tuition provider: it is generally possible to study independently and just pay the exam entry fees to your institute. However, the exams are not easy and it is important to think about how you prefer to study and to look carefully at the support and resources offered by different tuition providers before making any decision on how to prepare for the exams: the cheapest option might not necessarily be the best one for you.

What if I fail the exams?

This need not be a disaster: many accountants do fail one or more papers on their way to eventual success.

Table 8 Pass rates

	ACCA	CIMA	CIPFA	ICAEW	ICAI	ICAS
Percentage of overall passes at the final exam	48 (47)	55 (54)	70 (71)	77 (79)	76 (83)	76 (74)
Percentage of those overall passes that were first-time passes	51 (52)	54 (60)	N/A	85 (61)	82 (74)	N/A

The figures above are for exam sittings in 2008 and (in brackets) 2007

There are many reasons for the pass and failure rates that lie behind these statistics. Pass rates can vary between individual exam papers, firms, tuition providers and between UK and overseas exam centres. Even students with very good academic backgrounds may find it a challenge to combine work and study, or to get to grips with accounting as a subject if they have never studied it before.

All the institutes will normally allow you a certain number of resits, but employers may not always be so accommodating. Some employers will only allow you one or two attempts at the exams and will terminate your contract if you are not successful. Others will allow you further resits, but these will have to be at your own expense.

If the worst does happen and you fail your exams repeatedly, it is still possible to use your work experience to make a career in accountancy. A number of employers advertise for 'part-qualified' or 'QBE' (qualified by experience) accountants to carry out tasks such as accounts preparation and producing reports.

Alternatively, you may find that your talents lie elsewhere. People who have begun their career in business as accountants but have not gained a professional qualification include successful entrepreneurs such as Hugh Corbett, founder of the Slug and Lettuce pub chain; Peter Dawe, who set up Pipex, the UK's first commercial internet provider, and Michael Heseltine (now Lord Heseltine), founder of Haymarket Media Group and Deputy Prime Minister 1995–97.

And somebody who could see the funny side of not passing accountancy exams is American comedian Bob Newhart, who worked as a bookkeeper for a large company in Chicago. 'Some people wonder if it isn't unusual for an accountant to become a comedian. It's unusual for a good accountant to become a comedian. I was a very poor accountant.'

SKILLS

There is more to being an accountant than passing exams. Employers will look for the following skills and competencies, which will be assessed throughout their recruitment process (see Chapter 6 for more about this).

Communication

Accountants must communicate with a variety of people, both orally and in writing. You will need to gather and pass on information from and to your colleagues and to clients (whether they are outside your own organisation or whether they work elsewhere within it). These clients will be represented by a wide range of people at all levels, from directors and senior managers to factory floor and warehouse personnel. Many of them (even at senior levels) will not have an understanding of accountancy and finance so it will be important that you can explain in plain English what you are doing and why it needs to be done, answer any questions they have and ask your own questions in a clear, tactful and diplomatic way.

Oral communication is important in building and maintaining good relationships with clients. Accountancy is not a career for the shy and retiring: you must be able to build a rapport quickly, to motivate other people and to have the confidence to question information where necessary.

Communication is a two-way process and listening is as important as speaking. The ability to pay attention to what you hear and to make sure that you have understood it correctly will help you to work effectively with other people.

Written communication skills are used in everything from emails and letters to detailed financial reports and advice. It is important to be able to express yourself clearly and to make sure that what may be complex ideas are accurately conveyed at an appropriate level for the reader.

Numeracy

This is obviously important for any accountant – but it doesn't mean a higher degree in mathematics, or the ability to perform calculations to 10 decimal places in your head. Computers and calculators do the detailed figure work: the accountant's job is to understand and interpret their results. You will need to be comfortable with figures and statistical data but, if you can work out your monthly spending, check your bank statement or make a rough calculation of your supermarket bill before you arrive at the checkout, these are good indications that you will be able to cope. Employers will usually look for a good grade at GCSE maths (or equivalent), or set a numeracy test as part of their selection process to confirm this.

Teamwork

Working in almost any accountancy role in any organisation demands the ability to co-ordinate your work with that of other people – sharing information, handling any problems that arise and helping each other out as needed. This is particularly important in audit work, where all but the smallest audits are carried out by teams rather than individuals. A typical audit team is made up of a group of people at different levels of experience, each of whom is given specific tasks or responsibilities but all of whom must work together to complete the audit.

Organisational skills

Accountants are continually working to deadlines: to complete audits or to produce monthly/quarterly reports, annual accounts or tax returns, for example. You must be able to manage your time in order to meet deadlines, plan and organise your own work and that of other people. On a personal level, time-management skills will also be needed to combine work and study while you are training, to prepare for the exams and to keep some kind of a social life going at the same time!

Even the best time-management plan sometimes goes wrong – you may get given a task at the last minute, a colleague may be off sick or the computer system may crash – so it is also important to take account of this when making your plans and not to panic in a crisis.

Attention to detail is also important in a profession where a misplaced decimal point can be worth many thousands of pounds, or a missed deadline can result in a large fine for your company or your client.

Problem solving/analysing

Accountants will use their skills and training to analyse information presented in figures and to interpret the meaning of these figures. This does not just involve following set procedures: lateral thinking, and the ability to look at a problem from a variety of angles, is often required. Accountants also need to be able to appreciate problems, and their potential solutions, from a non-accountant's perspective so that they can advise clients and perhaps help to prevent similar problems cropping up again.

Integrity

Accountants are responsible for dealing with other people's money and are given access to confidential financial information. It is therefore essential that they should be absolutely honest and trustworthy. Accountants are required by their professional associations to comply with relevant laws and regulations and to avoid doing anything that might bring the profession into discredit. The Rehabilitation of Offenders Act specifically excludes accountants, so an employer must ask for details of all past convictions, even 'spent' ones, and also a Criminal Records Bureau check. This will not necessarily exclude anyone with a criminal record (depending on the nature of the offence) from becoming an accountant, as each case will be considered on an individual basis, but it is essential to declare it.

Commercial awareness

This can be summed up as an interest in business and an understanding of the wider environment in which an organisation operates – its customers, competitors and suppliers, for example. This awareness is not restricted to profit-making organisations: public sector bodies, charities and professional bodies are all affected by the activities of the business and financial world and work under many of the same pressures. Accountancy does not exist in a vacuum – many clients look to their accountant not only for accountancy services but also for general business advice.

Flexibility

Your role and responsibilities will change as your career progresses, so you must be prepared to cope with change. At the start of your career, you are likely to have to carry out some low-level and routine work, even if you are a graduate, and should show a positive attitude to this. Client service is at the heart of private practice firms – without clients, they would have no work – so you must be ready to go out of your way to help and advise clients and to meet their demands (even if these sometimes seem unreasonable!).

IT skills

Accountants make use of many specialised programs for handling accounting records and other financial information. While you will normally learn these during your training, applicants are usually expected to be able to make use of the basic Microsoft Office programs. A knowledge of spreadsheets (such as MS Excel) is particularly useful, as these are the main tool used by accountants for storing and handling financial data.

Self-presentation

This is especially important when you are meeting clients. Even if you are in a very junior role at the start of your career, you will be seen as the representative of your company or your department, and must come across as credible and confident. This means a smart appearance, a professional attitude and good social skills.

Motivation and commitment

Qualifying as an accountant will require a lot of hard work and study. Often, you will be employed in a full-time job while studying in your own time. Your employer will usually monitor your training and offer support, but will still expect you to take responsibility for your own learning and to ask for any help that you feel you need. This takes determination and the ability to keep yourself motivated even when things do seem difficult.

Chapter Five
WORKING IN ACCOUNTANCY: AS A TRAINEE

Chapter 3 of this book looked at some of the range of roles and specialisations that a career in accountancy can offer. Many of these, though, will only be open to you once you have gained a good grounding in the basics of accountancy. This chapter focuses on what life is like as a trainee accountant: the work that you will be doing, your working environment and how your work is likely to develop as your career progresses. Chapter 7 will look at the work of qualified accountants and how your career might develop once you reach this stage.

As you read this chapter, keep in mind that, alongside your work as a trainee, you will also be spending a considerable amount of time studying towards your professional exams.

WHAT SORT OF WORK WILL I BE DOING WHEN I START OUT IN ACCOUNTANCY?

You can expect a steep learning curve when you first start working in accountancy. Although your employer will usually provide a basic induction training, their aim is to get you into real work as soon as possible and your induction may last no more than one week. Much of your training and development will take place on the job.

The specific tasks that you will be doing will depend on your employer and the training programme they have designed for you but, as a general guide, some of the most common tasks for trainees include the following.

In private practice

- **Basic bookkeeping tasks:** analysing ledgers and ensuring that accounts balance.

- **Preparing accounts** using the client's records.

- **Assisting on audits,** carrying out tests and checks to establish the accuracy of the accounts. Much of this work involves taking samples of records such as invoices and receipts and checking them against the information about that transaction entered on a spreadsheet.

- **Stocktaking:** this involves verifying that stock physically exists and is owned by the client. This may be done by a full count or by sampling, depending on the amount and nature of the stock.

- **Checking documentation** relating to a client's tax affairs and using this information to complete VAT and income tax returns.

Jodie is a first-year trainee at the Cambridge office of PricewaterhouseCoopers LLP.

'Accountancy was definitely a change of direction for me – I worked as a contemporary dancer for four years before doing a degree in psychology at York University. I then decided on a career in business and looked at accountancy, management consultancy and human resource management. I chose accountancy because I felt the ACA would be recognised by the broadest range of employers, not just accountancy firms, and would give me the best possible grounding in business.

'I have now been with PricewaterhouseCoopers for five months and study and exams have taken up most of my time so far – almost half of my first year will be spent at college.

I also study in the evenings for up to three hours during college time, and up to one hour a night while I'm working. I have taken six exams so far, of which law was by far the most challenging, so I was really pleased when I passed it!

'Because of the amount of time given to study and exams, I have worked on relatively few clients so far, but have still been involved in a number of stock counts – this is something you do pretty regularly as a first year. I have counted tuna, rice, meat, X-ray machines, medical equipment and chemicals. The count at a meat storage facility was my worst experience so far – it was −25°, which really is cold!

'I was surprised by how much time is spent out at client sites – I expected I would spend half my time with clients and half in the office, but the split is more like 80:20. When I'm working at a client site I usually get there by 8.30 a.m. Sometimes they are quite far from home so then it's an early start to beat the morning traffic. So far, I have spent each new week at a new client, so I have had to adapt very quickly to their way of working and work hard to build good client relationships. Usually, a more senior member of our audit team will be my "coach" and they will talk me through the tasks I have been assigned for the week. The tasks themselves are varied: one day I might be looking at assets to see whether they do in fact exist, another I might be testing payroll. At the end of the day, I have a brief catch up with my team and we discuss any issues before heading home. So far I have been lucky and haven't had to do much overtime.

'Accountancy is challenging, varied and interesting and I hope that in five years' time I will still be working with PricewaterhouseCoopers. I would love to do a secondment, either abroad or to a different service within the firm, and I also hope that by that time I will be on my way to becoming a manager. Although I have a long way to go yet, I've already learned so much in such a short time!'

Accountancy firms tend to be quite hierarchical but, since the hierarchy is based on experience and qualifications, responsibility does come quickly. Once you have passed the first stage of your professional exams, which could be within six months to a year after joining the firm, you could be planning and carrying out small assignments on your own. This will involve you in more direct contact with clients, although a qualified accountant will have overall responsibility for the audit. Other tasks at this stage could include:

- starting to work with owners, managers and directors rather than just with accounts staff
- completing and finalising accounts prepared by more junior trainees
- supervising and supporting junior trainees
- working with larger clients and more complex issues
- becoming involved in advising clients on their tax affairs and working out tax liabilities
- responsibility for compliance with accounting standards and quality benchmarks.

This sets the pattern for the remainder of your training: your work increases in quantity and complexity, you are given a higher level of responsibility and work more closely with clients at senior levels, advising clients directly on many issues. In large firms, you may begin to specialise in a particular type of client (such as banks, energy companies or charities) or a particular type of work, such as tax or insolvency – this may be through a short placement, typically lasting three or four months, in a specialist department, which gives you a taste of the work and a chance to try it out before you qualify.

> *In your second year, you start to get more involved in the technical side of the audit – analysis and compliance. This involves making sure that the client is adhering to legal accounting requirements and standards and considering whether the figures in the accounts are logical and likely on the basis of all the information that you have about the client's activities. You don't leave testing behind completely, but you are more likely to be overseeing the tests rather than doing them yourself.*
>
> *Trainee in a large London firm*

In industry, commerce and the public sector

Trainees in these areas will normally gain experience in both financial and management accounting, although they may then go on to specialise in just one of these areas as their career progresses.

Financial accounting

- **Accounts payable:** dealing with invoices from suppliers, tax returns, travel expenses and similar items.

- **Accounts receivable:** invoicing customers for goods or services supplied to them, handling receipts.

- **Payroll administration:** dealing with wages and salaries.

- Preparation and maintenance of **financial accounts**.

- **Reconciling accounts** on a weekly or monthly basis to ensure that any errors can be picked up and put right as soon as possible.

- **Preparing balance sheets** and financial statements.

- **Preparing files and documents for external audits** and assisting the auditors with any queries.

- Completing corporate **tax and VAT returns**.

Management accounting

- **Preparing management accounts.**

- **Monitoring costs** and comparing them against budgets.

- **Collecting and analysing data** and using it to produce reports and forecasts. This may be on a regular basis, for example a monthly review of sales, or for a one-off report on a specific issue or problem.

- Carrying out **research** to contribute to projects.

- Performing **financial health checks** on companies bidding for contracts.

At the start of your career in these areas, most of your time is likely to be spent on accounting and reporting tasks such as those above. As your career progresses, your work will involve more analysis and planning. This will often take the form of ad hoc projects rather than routine and recurring assignments, which will bring greater variety to your work. These projects will involve working independently or in a small team to solve problems or to consider new developments and their financial implications. Project work will often involve working under pressure and to deadlines, and you will have contact with people throughout your organisation and with external bodies in order to gather the information you need and get input from non-accountancy staff. Examples of such project work could include:

- assessing the viability of new products or services

- implementing new government policies on education, healthcare or social services

- analysing the costs and benefits of investing in a new IT system

- looking at ways of cutting your organisation's costs by reducing waste or saving energy.

Management accountants also have a key advisory role in their organisation, providing information for managers in other departments that helps them to evaluate the financial consequences of their decisions. This could involve providing forecasts and reports showing the impact of different options being considered by managers in relation to, for example, the price of a product, recruiting new staff or leasing premises.

WHAT IF I HAVE TROUBLE UNDERSTANDING THE WORK?

There will be help available! Larger organisations will have a mentoring or 'buddying' system, and you will be able to go to a specific individual for informal advice about any aspect of your work, study or training. But even if your employer doesn't offer this, don't be afraid to ask for help. It's better to ask what may seem like a stupid question than to plough on regardless and create a big mess that will take time and trouble to sort out.

WHO WILL I BE WORKING WITH?

In large organisations, you will be one of a number of trainees – most of them recent graduates and all going through similar training programmes. This makes it a bit like being back at university, surrounded by people of similar ages and interests – but, like university, you are there to study and, unlike most university students, you have to study while doing a demanding full-time job as well!

In a smaller firm or department, you may be the only trainee and may be working with colleagues who are mostly quite a bit older than yourself. You may feel isolated and inadequate when you compare your colleagues' knowledge and experience with your own. Remember that they too were in the same position once and that it won't take you long to learn.

As well as your colleagues in your firm or department, you will also have a great deal of contact with external clients and with people from other departments.

If you are working in audit for a large or large/medium firm, your main point of contact with clients will be their in-house accountants. This can be very helpful, as they will know how everything works in their company and, like you, will be keen to make sure that the audit runs as quickly and smoothly as possible. In smaller firms, you are likely to have more dealings with owner-managers and self-employed business people and professionals. They too are usually pleasant to work with as they will appreciate your help with things (such as accounts and tax returns) which they see as complicated and unwelcome distractions from their real business.

At times, you will meet people who are less co-operative, who may resent your coming in to ask them questions and who may react with suspicion – people often fear that auditors are 'out to get them' in some way. You will need good people skills to put people at their ease and to get the information from them that you need to do your job effectively.

WHAT ARE THE WORKING HOURS LIKE?

These are usually quite regular – while you may not work exactly nine to five, you won't usually need to start or finish more than an hour or so

before or after these times. But accountancy is full of deadlines –
for completing audits, month-end accounts, tax returns or projects –
and you may need to work longer hours in the run-up to these
deadlines.

As a general rule, larger employers are likely to demand longer working
hours, especially if they are multinational and need to co-ordinate the
work of staff in different time zones. This can involve working well into the
night on occasions.

Employers do want their trainees to qualify as soon as possible and
will try not to assign you to big or important jobs that conflict with
your study or exam commitments. Even so, there will be times when
your day-to-day work, or the demands of clients, needs to take priority
over your study. This seems to happen particularly often in industry
and, although you will be given the chance to make up the study
time at a later date, it could affect the length of time that it takes
you to qualify.

> *January is our busiest time of year in the tax department, as HMRC's*
> *deadline for filing personal tax returns is 31 January. A lot of people*
> *put off thinking about their tax return until the last minute, and we*
> *always get a lot of new clients coming in just after Christmas.*
>
> *Trainee in a large regional firm*

WILL I HAVE TO WORK IN AN OFFICE?

You probably will spend a lot of your time in an office – but it may not
always be the same office. Audit trainees in private practice may spend
less than half their time at the offices of their employer but will be based
at their client's premises. These premises are not just offices – you may
find yourself checking stock in a factory, a car dealership, a publishing
house or even a racing stables.

Tax trainees, and accountants in industry, commerce and the public
sector, will spend more time in their own offices but will get out of them
regularly to talk to colleagues in other departments.

Emma is a second-year trainee at PKF.

'After graduating in archaeology, I moved to London to start a job in advertising sales, but soon found out that sales wasn't for me and joined the training team at PKF in an admin role. From there, I found that I was interested in moving into accountancy myself, as I would get to use my brain every day in a challenging, fast-paced and interesting industry. So I applied for the graduate scheme within PKF and am now in my second year of training.

'You get a good variety of clients when you work at PKF as we have a large range of client types and sizes – it's good for helping you to determine where your interests lie. I've worked on a lot of corporate audits, for a variety of different clients, mainly in the automotive industry, mining or property. I've done public sector work for a church and a museum, a government department and a number of local councils. One of the clients I work on is a Premier League football club. As a huge sports fan myself, I loved being able to see how the club runs day to day and how things like the transfer market work. The finance department is also located at the training ground, which makes the job really interesting, as the audit room overlooks the pitch.

'I've also done some work for a couple of councils on the south coast, which was another great experience. The people I worked with were all really friendly – one member of the finance team drove me around the towns to check some fixed assets and gave me a scenic tour and a mini history lesson whilst we did the work. They also take on board all the suggestions you make so you can see that the work you've done has been productive.

'Not all client work is quite as enjoyable – I once had to work at a crematorium. The finance department were really nice, but it was certainly a subdued atmosphere, especially as we could hear funerals taking place outside the office we were in.

'The other thing I don't enjoy is the exams! I knew that the study would be hard work, but I still wasn't fully prepared for how intensive the weeks in college are. It really is incredibly hard work, and very tiring when you are preparing for exams. The worst experience I have had so far is probably sitting TPS – the second stage of the ICAS qualification. It's incredibly intensive and by the end of the course you end up exhausted and very stressed. The feeling when you finish your last exam is fantastic, though!

'Accountancy has surprised me in that I enjoy it so much – I thought it would be a good, safe career choice that I would find interesting, but I like my job more than I ever thought I would! I've made some brilliant friends too, and I never expected to find such a good social aspect to the job – the people I work with here really make going to work enjoyable.'

WILL I HAVE TO WEAR A SUIT?

It's not for nothing that accountants are often referred to as 'the suits' – they usually have to dress smartly and conservatively. This is especially true in firms, where you will be expected to present a professional appearance to clients (although visits to some clients' operations may offer the chance to set off your business suit with a fetching hard hat or pair of wellies). In in-house accounting departments, you may be able to wear 'business casual' dress for your day-to-day work, although you will still need a suit or two in your wardrobe to wear to business meetings.

It's not just your clothes that should conform to a dress code – you won't find many accountants with pink hair or a pierced nose.

WILL I NEED TO TRAVEL?

Working in audit with larger accountancy firms is likely to involve quite a bit of travelling. Their clients may be quite widely scattered and the audits of large clients may take a month – or even more – in which case your firm will put you up in a hotel for the duration of the audit. This travel is usually within the UK, although trainees do occasionally get the opportunity to travel abroad. This is not usually as exciting as it sounds – you are unlikely to see anything of the country you visit but the airport and the office!

Tax specialists and in-house accountants are less likely to need to travel on a regular basis, although, if you work for a large organisation with multiple sites, this may be a requirement.

Roberto, international graduate finance trainee at Heineken.

case STUDY

Although he did not do an accounting or business degree, Roberto learned about business and basic accountancy through working part time in his family's company. As a graduate, though, he wanted to get an insight into business on a larger scale and decided that a graduate training programme with an international company would give him the best grounding for the sort of business career that he wanted. When he searched for a suitable scheme by typing 'international graduate programme' into Google, Heineken came up near the top of the results and was exactly the type of company he was looking for. Their International Graduate Programme offers a range of career paths, including marketing, human resources and supply chain, but Roberto chose to specialise in finance, considering that this would be the best way to see all aspects of how a major company operates.

Heineken's International Graduate Programme is different from most other graduate schemes in offering four six-month placements, each in a different country and each involving work in a different area of finance. Roberto is spending his first six months in Madrid, after which he will move to Vienna, Edinburgh and another country, yet to be decided.

Another highly unusual aspect of the Heineken finance scheme is that, because of its diverse and international nature, graduates do not start to study for a professional qualification until after they have completed the programme. Roberto could then move back to the UK for the next stage in his career and take the professional exams of one of the UK accountancy bodies. In the meantime, Heineken has an online 'finance academy' allowing staff to study anything from introductory accounting courses to specific topics such as the individual International Accounting Standards, so that Roberto's learning is based around what he needs for his current project rather than following a fixed syllabus.

Roberto's role in his first placement is developing a financial planning tool – an IT system to help with budgeting and forecasting. Since it will be used throughout the finance function, a great deal of consultation with people from every part of this function is needed to assess what they want from this tool and to gather information that can be taken into account when designing it.

The tool is being developed by a small group of Heineken finance staff – up to director level – and external consultants. Roberto is the most junior member of this group but is given quite a lot of responsibility and is fully involved in the many meetings that are required to gather the information needed. This helps him to learn how other departments work and to get to know people throughout the business.

Roberto's next placement is likely to be in Vienna, involving internal audit of Heineken companies throughout Europe.

Another of the finance graduate trainees is already working there and travels extensively to visit different companies. Unlike Madrid, where Roberto (who is bilingual) works entirely through Spanish, the work in this office is carried out in English. Heineken does, though, provide German lessons to help graduates adapt to daily life in Vienna.

Finance has lived up to his expectations as a way of learning about business – 'it is such an interesting area and you learn so much from it about core areas of business. Whatever your role in business, you will need some financial knowledge and will need to appreciate how the work that you do affects the finances of the business. The more you know about finance, the better – it can only benefit your work!'

HOW MUCH WILL I BE PAID?

Accountancy may be a career that revolves around money, but you won't always earn as much of it as you might hope when you start out!

A typical starting salary on a graduate training scheme with a major employer would be around £24,000 – more with the very large employers, some of whom may also offer graduates a joining bonus (known as a 'golden hello'). Smaller employers, though, may pay under £20,000. Salaries also vary according to which part of the country you are working in.

Table 9 sets out some of the salaries offered by an assortment of employers in a variety of locations for trainee posts advertised during 2009.

Most employers will award trainees a salary increase for every stage of the professional exams that they complete – this could be up to £1,000.

Table 9 Starting salaries offered to trainees in industry, commerce, the public sector and private practice

Type of employer	Qualification	Location	Requirements	Salary
Consultancy	AAT/CIMA	Scotland	At least Highers	£12–15K
Private practice	AAT, ACA or ACCA	Kent and London	Some previous experience	£12–18K
Private practice	ACA	Oxfordshire	Graduate	£15K
Private practice	ACA or ACCA	Hertfordshire	Graduate	£16–18K
Private practice	AAT	London	A level or degree	£17,675
Manufacturing company	CIMA	North-West England	Graduate	£17K
Borough council	CIPFA	South-East England	'Preferably a graduate'	£17–18K
Private practice	ACCA	Surrey	Graduate	£18K
Private practice	ACA	Kent	Graduate	£19K
Private practice	CIPFA	Edinburgh	Graduate	£20K
Private practice	ACA	London	Graduate	£21K
Publishing company	ACCA or CIMA	London	Graduate	£21K
University	CIMA	London	Graduate	£23K
London borough	CIPFA	London	Graduate	£23K
Retailer	CIMA	Leeds	Graduate	£23K
Computer manufacturer	ACCA or CIMA	Scotland	Graduate	£23.5–26K

(Continued)

Type of employer	Qualification	Location	Requirements	Salary
Private practice	ACA	London/ South-East England	Graduate	£24K
Private practice	CIPFA	London	Graduate	£25K
Government department	ACA, ACCA, CIMA or CIPFA	London	Graduate	£25K
Energy company	CIMA	South-East or North-West England	Graduate	£25K
IT services	ACCA or CIMA	South-East England	Graduate	£26.5K
Railway company	ACCA or CIMA	All UK	Graduate	£24.5K + £3K 'welcome bonus'
Media company	CIMA	London, Hampshire or Leeds	Graduate	£26K + £2K joining bonus
Private practice	ACA	London	Graduate	£27K
Insurance company	ACA	Norfolk	Graduate	£27.5K + joining bonus
Investment bank	ACA, ACCA or CIMA	London	Graduate	£29K
Regulatory body	CIMA	London	Graduate	£29K + £2.5K joining bonus
Confectionery company	CIMA	Various locations	Graduate	£31K

ARE THERE ANY OTHER BENEFITS?

The main benefit will be paid study leave and financial support for your study and exams – this could be worth around £5,000 on top of your salary and other benefits. These other benefits will vary according to your employer, but may include pension schemes, health insurance, season ticket loans and/or subsidised leisure facilities. The larger your employer, the more likely you are to be offered a range of such benefits.

HOW LONG WILL IT TAKE ME TO QUALIFY AS AN ACCOUNTANT?

If you come into accountancy as a school leaver, the AAT and equivalent qualifications will usually take two years to complete. You can then move on to become a student of one of the chartered accountancy bodies and from this point could become qualified in as little as two more years. If you join the profession as a graduate, whatever your degree subject, it will take you a minimum of three years to complete your exams and experience – most people qualify successfully within three to four years.

Once you qualify, there are many opportunities open to you. Chapter 7 looks at these and at how your career might progress as a qualified accountant.

Chapter Six

FINDING YOUR FIRST ROLE

If you have read this far, you must feel that accountancy is the right career for you and that you are the right sort of person to succeed in it. So how do you go about putting your career ambitions into practice?

AN INSIDE VIEW

It's always helpful to get some first-hand insight into a career before you begin to make applications for your first professional role. Not only will this help you to be absolutely sure that you have made the right choice, but it will help you with those applications as well.

There are many ways in which you can get this insight, both through formal schemes and informal approaches. Work experience does not have to be a structured work placement or a paid internship – work shadowing can be just as useful a way of finding out what it is like to work in accountancy.

Start with the professional bodies. Their websites will have lists of employers, often offering work experience placements as well as trainee positions. Some institutes have a network of local careers advisers – practising accountants who you can approach for advice about your carer or for answers to any questions you have.

If you are still at school, your school may be able to arrange for you to do a short work experience placement in accountancy. These usually take place at some point during Year 10 or 11.

Some degrees in accounting and finance, or in business more generally, include a 'year in industry' placement. This doesn't have to be in 'industry' as such – you could spend it in an accountancy firm, a manufacturing or service company or a public sector body. During this year, you will be employed by that organisation, you will be earning a salary and doing work very similar to that of a first-year trainee accountant – you may even be able to take some of the first-stage professional exams. At the end of the year in industry, you will return to university to complete the final year of your degree. After graduating, many people return to the organisation where they spent their placement year to pick up their work and training where they left off – but if you don't feel that this is the right option for you, there is absolutely no obligation to return. You are free to look for any job anywhere else and, whether or not that job is in accountancy, the experience you have gained will have given you valuable skills and experience to help you stand out from other graduates.

Chris, trainee chartered accountant and former placement student.

Chris's degree in accounting and finance included a one-year sandwich placement which he spent working for Reeves+Neylan LLP, a large regional firm in the South-East. After graduating in 2009 he returned to the firm as a chartered accountancy trainee.

Chris's placement year was split into two parts, covering tax and audit work. Following a short in-house course covering the basics of accounts, taxation and the firm's procedures, he began working in the tax department, helping to prepare tax returns for individual clients, such as landlords, professionals and self-employed people. His main tasks involved:

■ writing to clients to request the information that HMRC would require from them

- checking items received from clients, such as statements of interest paid on investments, or records of rental income from properties, against the firm's checklist of required items
- contacting clients when necessary to obtain further documentation or to clarify any queries
- entering data into the clients' tax returns.

This part of the placement lasted from August until the end of January and so covered the busiest time of year for personal tax accountants. Chris then moved on to the corporate services department, where he worked on the audit of a number of companies including a construction firm, a pharmaceutical company and a company that, although based in the UK, traded in France and therefore produced all its documentation in French.

As the junior member of the audit team, usually working with two or three more senior staff, Chris was responsible for carrying out a lot of 'walk-through testing'. This involves checking systems and procedures at every stage of a process – for example, testing a sales system in this way would be done by checking the progress of a sample item through the system – ordering, invoicing, delivery notes, entry in the sales ledger and payment into the company's bank account.

Audit work therefore involves getting to know the client's system. Different clients have different systems and only by gaining an understanding of how a particular client's systems work can the auditor work out the best way to test them. This can mean asking a lot of questions, which some clients can view as a nuisance – Chris, though, has always found the clients that he works with to be friendly and helpful. As he is dealing with companies of a reasonable size, he is working with in-house accountants who appreciate the need for an audit and know what is expected of them.

Following his placement, Chris was offered an ACA training contract and returned to the firm after completing his degree. The placement year had given him a good opportunity to get to know the firm and its clients and he wasn't tempted to look at any other firms but enjoyed the security of having a job awaiting him at the end of his final year at university.

As a trainee, Chris is currently working again in corporate services and has begun to study for the ICAEW exams, attending a local college for periods of two weeks at a time every few months. Although his degree gives him the maximum number of exemptions from these exams, and much of the study in the first six months has recapped his previous study, he has still found it useful to attend the classes and to study accountancy from a more 'practical' perspective.

The remainder of Chris's training contract will involve work in accounting, audit and tax services. Once he qualifies, he will be able to choose an area of specialisation and may decide then to take a further qualification in tax. For the moment, though, he is keeping his options open and feels that Reeves+Neylan LLP is an ideal place to train, as a top 50 firm with a wide range of work but not so big as to be impersonal – the partners know all the trainees by name and the firm has a friendly and supportive working environment.

Most university graduates who go into accountancy, though, have not done a year in industry and a very large number of them have not studied a subject related in any way to accountancy or to business. Students of any subject are welcome to apply for vacation schemes with accountancy firms and other major graduate recruiters and can get experience in this way. These schemes range from short 'insight' days to three-month summer placements working alongside accountants and other employees. Some are open to students in their first year; others will only take applications from students in their second or final year.

Your university careers service will be able to help you to find employers offering these schemes.

Networking is a very effective way for anybody interested in an accounting career to start to find out more about it and it can be used at any stage of your career planning – at school, at university or as a career changer. At its simplest, networking is using personal contacts to find out more about an area of work that interests you. You may feel that you don't have any contacts in accountancy at this stage, but you don't have to limit yourself to your own contacts. Somebody that you know probably knows an accountant – remember, everybody needs accountants! If any of your family or friends are self-employed, ask them who does their accounts. If they work in a large organisation, ask them if they can put you in touch with someone in the accounts department there. Once you have a first point of contact, you can ask them about their work and get first-hand advice; you may even be able to arrange some informal work experience.

You can also start to create your own network by approaching potential employers direct. Use the professional bodies' websites, local business directories or the *Yellow Pages* to find accountancy firms and then approach them to ask for work experience. If this isn't available, they may be willing to allow you to work-shadow: to spend a day following somebody in the firm as they go about their regular work.

FINDING OUT MORE

Whatever first-hand experience you can get, it is likely that you will still only manage to get exposure to a small part of the accountancy profession, so you should continue to use other resources to find out more about this career.

Schools, colleges and universities often arrange careers presentations where students can hear from accountants about their work and professional training. These may be organised by careers services, student societies or academic departments.

The professional bodies are also active in providing information about the careers to which their qualification might lead. You may be able to sign up to a programme such as the ACCA Accelerate scheme which provides information and advice about careers and employers and organises career-focused events for members.

WHEN TO APPLY FOR JOBS IN ACCOUNTANCY

Many employers of trainee accountants – accountancy firms, large companies and public sector organisations – work on an annual cycle when recruiting graduates and/or school and college leavers to train as accountants. You may need to apply as early as October or November to give yourself the best possible chance of being selected for a training scheme starting the following September. While many of these employers will keep recruiting well into the spring of each year – and maybe into early summer – the earlier you apply, the more vacancies will be available. You will also show keenness and motivation by applying earlier rather than later!

FINDING EMPLOYERS AND VACANCIES

The professional bodies are the best place to start – as well as lots of information on the qualifications they offer, they will have lists of employers offering trainee positions.

These lists are not the only way to find a first post in accountancy, though. The professional bodies that represent members in practice (ICAEW, ICAS, ICAI and ACCA) have comprehensive lists or directories of firms on their websites. Not all of these will recruit trainees – these lists are aimed at clients looking for accountancy services – but, as they can be searched by location or specialisation, they are useful for job-seekers too, especially if you aim to work for a smaller employer or are looking for work in a restricted geographical area.

If, on the other hand, you want to work for a large firm, the Accountancy Age website publishes an annual survey of the top 100 firms, with links to their websites and background reports on the top 50.

If you are an undergraduate or recent graduate there are many graduate sites such as Prospects, Milkround, Inside Careers and Target Jobs. As well as a good deal of general careers advice, they carry details of all kinds of graduate training programmes, including training contracts in accountancy firms and finance graduate training schemes in industry, commerce and the public sector.

Recruitment agencies may be another option. Some specialise in finance and accountancy roles: these may offer opportunities for trainees, but many of the posts they advertise will ask for at least six months' experience. They may not therefore be the best option when you are looking for your **first** role, but can be useful if you are moving on during your training.

There are also recruitment agencies that specialise in opportunities for recent graduates. These usually cover vacancies for all kinds of jobs: some of them are likely to be in accountancy and these may not require previous experience.

WHAT ROLES TO APPLY FOR

Your first role could be as a trainee accountant on a formal programme of work, study and on-the-job training leading to one of the qualifications awarded by the professional accountancy bodies. Your employer may give you a free choice as to which institute you join, or may have a link to one particular institute. In accountancy firms, this programme usually takes place under a 'training contract', while other types of organisation may refer to it as an 'accountancy training scheme' or 'finance training scheme'. These posts may be advertised as 'trainee accountant', 'trainee chartered accountant', 'trainee management accountant', etc.: the word 'trainee' in the job title is an obvious sign that this is an entry-level position, but you will need to check what particular educational requirements the employer has set for the post. A number of trainee posts will specify, or give preference to, graduate applicants and there may also be additional degree class or subject area requirements.

While very many accountants do start as trainees, with their employment linked to their professional training from the beginning, this is not the only way to become an accountant. You could also join an accountancy firm or an accounts department in a junior role and develop your career through experience and/or through studying independently. Your employer may agree to provide support for your study once you have been with them for a reasonable length of time.

There are many different job titles used for these junior roles: some are very general, such as 'accounts clerk' and 'accounts assistant'; others may relate to a more specific role such as 'purchase ledger clerk'. You do need to check the person specification carefully for these job titles, as firms use them in different ways and they do not always mean that the job is a suitable one for a new entrant to accountancy.

WHAT TO LOOK FOR IN AN EMPLOYER

Don't start with a list of employers and work through them from A to Z. Think about what you want from your career and your working environment and narrow down the potential employers to those who best fit with your preferences. Here are some of the factors that may be significant.

Location

Do you want to work near your home, stay in your university town or work in a big city? Opportunities to work in accountancy can be found almost anywhere, but if you have a strong preference for one location above all others, this will help to narrow down your opportunities. If it narrows them down too much, think about how much travelling or commuting you would be prepared to do.

Qualifications offered

Does an accounting firm offer you the chance to study for ACA/CA, ACCA or AAT qualifications – or all three? Does a company offer ACCA, CIMA or ACA? Public sector employers do not just offer the CIPFA qualification – many offer ACCA, CIMA and/or ACA as well. Are any other qualifications available? Which one would be best for you? What support does the employer offer for your study and professional exams?

Size

How big is the organisation? Is it growing, and if so, how fast? Does it have other offices or branches where you might work as your career develops? Does it have an international network of offices or associated companies?

What do they do?

If it is an accountancy firm, who are its clients? If it is another type of organisation, does it manufacture goods (and, if so, what does it make)?

Does it provide a commercial service? Is it in the public or voluntary sector? What is its main area of business or activity?

What are the career prospects with this employer?

Some employers pride themselves on recruiting trainees who will stay with them and become future senior managers or partners. This may be what you are looking for if location is important to you, although a long-term career can never be guaranteed. Other employers, particularly the major chartered accountancy firms, recruit large numbers of trainees and don't expect all of them to stay with the firm after they qualify. This is not a disadvantage – the experience you have gained with these firms, and their reputation, will normally make you attractive to all kinds of other employers, and the option to stay with the firm that has trained you will also be there if you choose. You may also want to look at how the experience and qualification that you would gain with this employer might be transferred elsewhere if you do move on.

What do they expect from candidates?

Some employers are very strict in their requirements for UCAS points or degree class. If you can't meet these requirements, and don't have any mitigating circumstances to help explain them, it is probably not worth applying to that employer – look for one that will be more flexible.

HOW TO APPLY

Different employers have different methods of application. While smaller employers will often ask you to send them a curriculum vitae (CV) and letter, most of the larger ones have their own application form. Some of these may be quite short and seemingly straightforward: others will include a number of more complex and demanding questions.

Whatever its style and format, an application form is not just designed to collect factual information, such as your qualifications and employment history. It will also include questions that will give the employer an indication of your interest in, and suitability for, a career in accountancy, such as:

- why do you want to be an accountant?
- why are you applying to this company?
- what do you expect to be doing during your first year of training?

There may be only one question like this on the application form, but it will nonetheless be the most important one!

Many large organisations design their application forms around the competencies that are needed to do the job well (the skills listed at the end of Chapter 4). These forms include a number of questions starting:

- 'describe a situation where you . . .'

- 'give an example of a time when you . . .'

The situations or examples that they ask you to outline typically include:

- setting yourself a goal and working towards achieving it

- working as part of a team

- dealing with a difficult problem

- managing a number of different tasks or activities at the same time.

These are all things that you will need to do in order to pass your accountancy exams and to succeed in your day-to-day work: if you can show that you have already done these things in different situations in the past, you will be able to show the employer that you have the potential to do them in your future career.

If you apply by means of a CV, the CV itself will principally include factual details about your education, qualifications and experience. However, you can still give the employer information about your reasons for applying to them, and the skills which you can offer them, in the covering letter you send with the CV.

WHAT EMPLOYERS LIKE TO SEE IN CVs AND APPLICATION FORMS

- A targeted application: one that shows that you have done your research and you know what the employer does, what they are looking for and what they can offer you.

- A candidate who knows why they want to become an accountant and can show why they would make a good accountant.

- Accuracy: no spelling mistakes or grammatical howlers.

- Clear and concise answers to the questions.

- A clearly laid out CV (when used) that makes it easy for the reader to pick out the key points.

- Some experience relevant to accountancy: although this doesn't have to be in accountancy itself. This could include:

  - taking part in a Young Enterprise programme

  - acting as treasurer for a club or society

  - work experience that has involved dealing with cash, such as a part-time job in a shop or restaurant.

- Involvement in activities outside education and employment, such as sports, hobbies and voluntary work. This demonstrates enthusiasm and motivation, and can also help your application stand out from all the others.

Top 10 mistakes in applications

1 Getting the employer's name wrong. Many accountancy firms do have rather odd or complicated names, so make sure that you spell them correctly!

2 Writing to an accountancy firm saying, 'I want to work for your company because . . .' Firms and companies are different legal entities and your application will look better if you show that you are aware of this!

3 Not knowing the difference between different types of firm and different types of accountancy, for example, mixing up ACA with ACCA or AAT with ATT.

4 Not answering questions in sufficient detail, or not answering the actual question that was asked. For example, if you are asked to describe a time when you worked as a member of a team, you should write about what **you** did and what you contributed to that team, not just about what the team as a whole did.

5   Giving false information. If a firm looks for high academic grades, and you don't have these, it is tempting to bump up your A level or degree results to the required standard in the hope of getting an interview – but don't! Your grades will be checked, either by asking your referee to confirm them or by asking you to provide copies of your certificates before you start work. If a 'mistake' of this nature is revealed, any job offer will be withdrawn – accountants have to be absolutely trustworthy.

6   Sending the same letter to lots of employers and forgetting to change the name of the employer in the letter!

7   Sending a CV when the employer has asked you to fill out an application form – or sending in an application form with 'See CV' written in every section

8   Using inappropriate paper for CVs and covering letters, such as bright pink paper or cheap lined paper from a memo pad.

9   Using a 'funny' email address such as mrturniphead@ yoohoo.com or boozysuzie@gogglemail.com. Employers may privately find your address just as hilarious as your friends do, but it won't encourage them to treat you as a serious candidate.

10   The biggest and most common mistake is **making too many applications**. Quality is better than quantity: it is better to spend several hours on one really good application than to spend the same amount of time on 20 badly done forms. If your application has not had sufficient time and thought put into it, this will show!

INTERVIEWS

Depending on the employer, an interview may be a cosy chat or a structured series of questions based on the competencies needed to do the job. Interviews with smaller employers are generally less formal than those with large firms and companies, which are the most likely to use competency-based questions.

Take an interest in current affairs, particularly business and finance-related developments: this is necessary for interviews, but it's also important because it will give you a better understanding of the issues facing your clients. Speak to as many people as you possibly can during your interviews – it's the best way to find out about that particular firm.

Trainee at a Big Four firm

Some questions you might be asked at an interview

■ Why have you chosen this qualification?

■ What other careers have you considered?

■ What do you feel would make you a good accountant?

■ Tell me about a time when you have:

■ worked under pressure

■ shown initiative.

■ Where do you see yourself in five years' time?

■ What do you know about this firm/company?

Tips for interview

■ Re-read your application before the interview: remind yourself what you have said and try to anticipate the questions that might come up.

■ Re-read the information you have about this organisation and remind yourself why you have applied to them. Interviewers appreciate candidates who are well informed and enthusiastic.

■ Dress smartly. Accountants are expected to present a professional image. Wear a suit and make sure that any tattoos are covered up and piercings removed (women can wear earrings, so long as they are not too large or distracting, but men would be best advised to remove these).

■   Make sure that you are up to date with business issues – one large accountancy firm regularly asks candidates if they read the *Financial Times*. Even if the FT is a bit daunting at this stage, you should follow business stories in the mainstream newspapers or news channels.

■   Think of some questions to ask the interviewer. These should be about training and career development rather than about pay and holidays!

■   Try and relax and be yourself.

Some questions you might ask the interviewer

■   How is the exam study organised?

■   How soon do you expect trainees to take their first set of exams?

■   How quickly could I complete all the exams?

■   What might I be doing during my first month in this job?

■   Who will I be working with?

■   What are the opportunities to move between departments to develop my experience?

■   Who will oversee my training and experience?

The websites and books listed in Chapter 8 will give you further advice on preparing for interviews and handling them successfully.

APTITUDE TESTS

Most big employers use numerical and verbal aptitude tests as part of their selection process. These may be taken on the day of the interview or you may be required to take them online before the interview stage.

You would expect employers to want to test your numerical reasoning skills, but the verbal reasoning tests are equally important as they assess your ability to understand and interpret written information.

Smaller organisations are less likely to use these tests and will rely on your exam results in maths and English to show them that you have these skills.

Aptitude tests often cause a great deal of anxiety, but are not as bad as many people fear! In particular, the numerical tests are not about abstract mathematical concepts but are more concerned with basic everyday arithmetic and being able to understand information presented in charts or graphs. Verbal reasoning tests usually ask you to read through paragraphs of text and then decide whether a number of statements relating to the information in the text are true or false.

It is possible, and highly advisable, to practise these tests in advance. If you haven't studied maths for a few years, you will find it useful to get back up to speed with procedures such as fractions and percentages. Even if you are studying maths at a high level, it will be useful to work through some practice tests: in the past, some maths graduates have been known to perform poorly in these tests because the questions seemed too simple and they therefore spent time looking for trick elements that weren't there! Your careers service will have a wealth of material on aptitude tests.

For tips on succeeding at aptitude tests and lots of practice papers see the Practice and Pass Professional series (*Verbal Reasoning Tests* and *Numeracy Tests*), published by Trotman.

ASSESSMENT CENTRES

Large organisations use a series of exercises to assess candidates, especially for graduate recruitment schemes. As well as interviews and aptitude tests, these assessment centres may include:

- **group exercises and discussions:** a small group of candidates works together to solve a problem

- **case studies:** you will be given a set of documents relating to a business issue to read and analyse and may then be asked to write a report based on the information in them or to present your conclusions orally

- **in-tray exercises:** you open an inbox with a series of messages and attached documents. You will need to read these through, decide which you need to act upon and in what order of priority, and draft replies to the most important

- **presentations:** either on a topic which you have had a chance to prepare before the interview or one given to you on the day.

Again, your careers service and www.prospects.ac.uk/links/ assessmentcntrs will be able to give you further information about assessment centres and to help you prepare for them.

JOB OFFERS

After working your way through all or some of these processes you will, if all has gone well, be offered a job!

Make sure that an offer is right for you before you accept it. Think back to the reasons that made you decide to apply to that employer – now that you have learned more about them, are you still as keen to work for them? In particular, consider the experience that you will gain and the training and support that you will receive. You may also want to think about what this position might lead to after you qualify and how it might influence your longer-term career prospects, but don't be too rigid about these at this stage – your plans may change over the next few years as you gain a greater insight into accountancy.

The salary offered may also be something to take into consideration, but shouldn't be your main reason for accepting a job: a slightly lower salary with a high level of support for your study is likely to be better than a higher salary but with less effort put into helping you to pass your exams. Don't be afraid to ask the employer more questions before you make a decision – or to ask to be put in touch with current trainees and get their advice.

Chapter Seven

YOUR FUTURE IN ACCOUNTANCY... AND BEYOND?

Accountancy is about qualifications and while you are training your attention will be focused on your twin goals of passing your exams and qualifying as an accountant. But once you have achieved these goals, what happens next?

This isn't a question that should be left until the day you qualify. It's worth taking time every so often during your training to think about your career plans, to look at the opportunities that will be open to you on qualification and to make sure that the experience you are currently gaining will help you to steer your career in the direction that you want it to go.

Your employer may encourage you to do this by organising regular meetings with a mentor who will encourage you to plan your career development, set yourself career goals and help you work towards them. They may also be able to help you to make sure that your training is structured in a way that allows you to focus on the area or areas that most interest you and build up relevant experience. In other organisations, especially smaller ones, the responsibility for your career planning will fall largely on your own shoulders.

Remember that, whichever of the professional institutes you train with, it will normally take a minimum of three years to become a fully qualified accountant. This gives you plenty of time to gain experience in different aspects of accountancy and by the time you qualify you should have gained a good insight into the various possibilities open to you.

Qualification is the start of a new phase in your career and is often seen as a chance to change direction and try out new fields of work. However, the choices you make at this time may have a significant impact on your long-term career, so they need to be thought through carefully.

With the workload and the amount of study expected of trainee accountants, it can be easy to overlook longer-term planning – but the earlier you start to think about these issues, the more likely you are to achieve your goals. Many employers will even ask you during your interview where you see yourself in five years' time!

Once you qualify, your options for your next step can be broadly summed up as follows:

- stay with your present employer

- move to a similar type of employer or role

- move to a different type of employer or role.

There are good reasons for and against all of these, and which is the 'best' option will depend very much on you as an individual as well as on your present and/or prospective employer.

YOUR NEXT STEP

Staying with your present employer

This may seem like the 'safe but boring' option, but this is not necessarily the case and there are a number of advantages.

If you have been employed under a training contract, or on a graduate training scheme, you are normally free to leave, should you wish to do so, at the end of your contract: technically, your contract may only last until the time you qualify. Similarly, your employer is not obliged to keep you on as a qualified accountant but, since this is the point where they really begin to benefit from all the training and development they have invested in you, they are usually more than happy for you to stay with them.

If you know that you want to move on in the not-too-distant future, but need further experience, or are waiting for the right opportunity to come up, staying with your first employer a little longer will usually be seen more positively by future employers than moving on somewhere where you may only stay a few months. Employers can be wary of what they see as 'job-hopping' and, even if you have good reasons for frequent moves, it is not always easy to explain these to a prospective new employer.

Also, as a newly qualified accountant, you are likely to be given a higher level of responsibility and will be able to build up experience at a more senior level. Even if you don't see yourself staying with your present employer in the long term, this will be helpful to you when you do feel ready to look for other positions. This experience may involve a higher level of client contact, taking greater responsibility for projects or supervision of other staff.

You may also be able to move into another department, a more specialised area of work or even to take up an international secondment.

The ICAEW's 2009 Career Benchmarking Survey found that half of their recently qualified members expected to gain promotion with their existing employer.

Chris is a senior accountant in the Business Services group at Ensors, a large regional firm in East Anglia.

case STUDY

'A career in accountancy is what I wanted to do ever since I realised I wasn't good enough to make it as a professional footballer! I'd always been good with maths and this career path was suggested to me during a meeting with a careers adviser at my high school. At the age of 15 I spent two weeks' work experience with an accountancy firm and knew then that it was the right job for me.

'I joined my current employer as an AAT trainee. As I had A levels, I started at intermediate rather than beginner level, so it took me two years to complete that qualification. I then opted to do my ACA exams and this took me a further three years. It wasn't all plain sailing – I messed up one exam along the way due to getting the timing wrong, and came out knowing that I'd failed. That was a pretty awful experience, but becoming ACA qualified in August 2009 was the best experience of my career so far. After putting in so much effort studying and sitting exams for five years, to be able to say I am a fully qualified chartered accountant is a fantastic feeling – made even better by the fact I may never have to sit another exam in my life!

'I work within Business Services, which deals with a vast range of clients, ranging from sole traders to limited companies. No day is the same and the variety of the work that I do is what keeps it interesting for me. One week I may be compiling the accounts for a taxi driver, the next week I could be working on an audit for a national haulage operator that has a multimillion-pound turnover. In the last couple of years I have specialised in preparing accounts for farming clients and performing independent examinations for solicitors. These are basically the same as audits for companies but specific to solicitors, and aim to ensure that money held on behalf of clients (for matters such as probate or conveyancing) has not been misused, and that the solicitors are complying with all the rules set out by the Solicitors Regulation Authority. I've also worked on the accounts of some famous celebrities – and got to meet them too!

'Once you qualify you get to have more responsibility with the work that you do until you get to a position where the partners of the firm are happy that your knowledge is of a sufficient level for you to be able to manage a client list of your own. This doesn't happen overnight, though, and I've only been qualified for six months! I do get the opportunity to have more communication with clients now, and managers are more confident in your ability to produce accounts with little or no supervision from them.

'Once you have an accountancy qualification it opens many doors for your career. I currently work in practice but would like to move into industry within the next five years, perhaps becoming a management accountant and eventually becoming a finance director. There are a number of job opportunities that an accountancy qualification can offer, whether it be ACA, ACCA, CIMA or any of the others and, as these qualifications are recognised worldwide, you even have the opportunity of working abroad – the world is your oyster!'

Your studying may not yet be over! If you decide to specialise, you may need to follow up your general accountancy qualification with one that is relevant to your chosen area, such as tax, insolvency or internal audit.

Finally, if you do feel that staying on with your first employer is the right option for you at this stage, this doesn't mean that you will need to stay with them forever. Many accountants move on between three and five years after they qualify, by which stage they have built up a significant amount of higher-level experience that makes them very marketable when the right time to move does arrive.

Moving to a similar employer

This may involve, for example, moving from one chartered accountancy firm, or one manufacturing company, to another where you will be working in a similar environment and, at least initially, on similar tasks, to those you would have done at your first employer.

So why move? It's true that some people only do so reluctantly: even if they would prefer to stay with the employer they trained with, this may not always be possible. Some employers recruit more accountancy trainees than they will need in the longer term, in order to allow for trainees failing their exams or choosing not to stay with them when they qualify. If these projections don't work out as planned, some newly-qualifieds may, through no fault of their own, be unable to stay on. Sometimes, an employer's position may have changed during the three years between a trainee joining them and qualifying and they may no longer have the opportunities that they originally expected to be able to offer.

Many other newly qualified accountants, though, choose to move, or are persuaded to move, elsewhere for more positive reasons. They may wish to move from a smaller firm to a larger one, or vice versa, in order to find a broader range of opportunities, or the chance to specialise in an area not available at their previous firm. They may wish to relocate geographically – within the UK or abroad. They may simply be seeking a higher salary.

If you are moving between firms in practice, you may be seeking exposure to a different range of clients. Larger firms may offer the chance to specialise in particular types of client and greater exposure to household-name clients, while smaller firms will offer closer involvement with clients such as smaller or owner-managed businesses. The nature of the clients you are working with may affect the issues involved in your day-to-day work – if you specialise in the charity sector, for example, you will be dealing with a different set of regulations and issues from those in the telecommunications sector.

In industry, commerce and the public sector, if you are moving at this stage to an organisation carrying out similar activities, you may do so because you see better future prospects with that employer or because it is more focused on an area of particular interest to you. You may, for example, have qualified with an electronics company but now want to bring your interest in cars into your work by transferring to a motor vehicle manufacturer. Accountancy is a skill that can be transferred across just about any areas of work: your qualification will be applicable whatever your employer's business actually involves.

Since accountancy has to work according to tightly defined standards, the differences between different employers do not lie so much in the nature of the work itself as in the working atmosphere and culture.

Moving to a different type of employer

This could involve, for example, moving from a chartered accountancy firm to a manufacturing company, from a manufacturing company to a public sector body or from a public body to an accountancy firm.

In industry and commerce, it could also involve moving to a company involved in a completely different area of business: for example, from a food manufacturer to a publishing company or from a bank to a retailer.

Career moves of this kind are not as unusual or as difficult as you might think. In particular, a qualification gained in private practice is readily transferable into industry and commerce or the public sector. Statistics show that, although the vast majority of chartered accountants have qualified in private practice, only about one-third of them stay in this sector in the longer term, with over 40% working in industry, commerce or the public sector.

The experience you have gained during your training in private practice, and the type of clients you have worked with, may influence your choice of employer or field of work if you are moving in this direction after you qualify.

Some people move into a different sector to broaden their experience before returning to their first area of work: it can be useful, for example, for accountants working in private practice to have gained a view of industry and commerce from the inside.

WHAT WILL YOUR WORK INVOLVE ONCE YOU QUALIFY?

As a recently qualified accountant, you could be:

- running audits or projects, from initial planning to the final report and presentation

- managing teams – allocating work, briefing the team, controlling the day-to-day work of team members, monitoring the team's work

- using your knowledge, experience and initiative to deal with queries and problems

- taking full responsibility for reporting, budgeting and forecasting

- liaising with clients at a higher level than previously

- reporting directly to senior management

- carrying out research, planning and investigations at a more advanced level and with wider responsibilities.

Matt is an insolvency administrator.

Matt is a recently qualified chartered accountant (ICAS) and has been working in the corporate recovery department of PKF, one of the top 10 accountancy firms, for five months.

Matt's degree was in electronic engineering and his first job after leaving university was as a graduate trainee with a company that engineers control systems for the oil and gas industry. As part of the graduate scheme, Matt got the opportunity to rotate around a number of departments, including sales and marketing. He became more interested in the business side of the company than in engineering its products and chose chartered accountancy training as a route into a career in business.

Matt's training, like that of most trainees at PKF, was in the assurance and advisory department, but completing his ICAS qualification opened up a wider range of possibilities in the firm. About three months before they qualify, PKF trainees take part in a two-day career development course where different departments make presentations to show the trainees what they have to offer.

This course, though, was not the main reason why Matt chose the corporate recovery department for his first post-qualification role. His interest in this area had begun at his first employer, which had gone through a difficult period and had been turned around and brought back into profit by a dynamic and enthusiastic managing director. Matt was fascinated by how this had been achieved and wanted to get involved in this process himself.

Working in corporate recovery is different from audit work in many ways. In particular, Matt needs to exercise a much higher degree of time management as he could be handling as many as 20 different cases at a time, while in audit it is possible to focus on just a single client. Also, audit work can be planned for well in advance, but insolvency work is much more unpredictable. Matt now spends much more time in the office, working with clients mostly over the phone, although he has also worked at some client sites, where the business is still trading and PKF have been appointed administrators of the company, and therefore are working with staff and liaising with customers and suppliers to rescue the company.

In the future, Matt would like to gain some experience in industry to help him towards his long-term goal of working in business recovery. He feels that this insight into industry from the inside, developing and running their accounting systems rather than just advising on them from an external point of view, will give him more credibility when advising clients. First, though, he needs to build up more experience in practice and plans to move back into audit to do this.

Matt feels that he has benefited from the greater variety of work and the friendly atmosphere at a large but non-Big Four firm. Audits at PKF tend to be smaller and shorter than they would at the Big Four, making the work more varied and giving exposure to a much wider variety of clients, such as companies, charities, venture capital firms, professional bodies and solicitors' firms. Most of the trainees who qualified at the same time as Matt have also stayed with PKF – 'there are so many opportunities to try different things within the firm when you qualify that it can be difficult to decide, but, whatever you choose, there is plenty of training available'.

If you hoped that the pressure would ease once your final exams were over, you may be disappointed! You may find that there are more demands made upon your time than there were when you were a student, now that you are able to devote yourself full time to your work rather than having to combine it with study.

Although your formal study may now be over (unless you choose to take an additional specialist qualification) you will still be expected to continue to develop your professional skills and knowledge. This, though, is less demanding than studying for the exams and is based more on experience than on formal study. A lot of what you learn in the natural course of your work, through briefings, discussions and mentoring, can therefore contribute towards your continuing professional development.

Another part of this professional development could be training courses provided by your employer. As well as introducing you to new technical aspects of accountancy, these often cover more general business skills such as team management, leadership and making presentations.

Three to five years after you qualify you could additionally be:

- preparing 'pitches' for new business: researching potential clients and preparing presentations to promote your firm's services to them

- planning audits: agreeing budgets and schedules with clients

- becoming more involved in strategic management and planning and having an active input into management decisions

- starting to specialise in one main area of work or type of client.

Most accountants don't specialise in any one area during their training, but once you are qualified you may want to use your general accountancy experience in a specialised area.

There are many opportunities to do this, either within the firm you have trained with or by moving to another employer that has a larger practice in this area. As with trainees, most firms will support their qualified staff in obtaining any further professional qualifications that will help them in their work.

As your career progresses, you may find yourself spending less time on technical accountancy work and more time on managing – people, projects, budgets or client relationships, for example. This wider experience is important if you want your career to reach a high level, as senior roles in accountancy carry a broad range of responsibilities and extend beyond accountancy itself.

HOW MUCH COULD YOU BE EARNING?

These figures are likely to be out of date well before you qualify, but will give a rough idea of what you might expect to earn at different stages of your career and in different roles.

Your salary will be affected by many factors, the main ones being the size of your employer, the type of employer you work for and your geographical location. These factors tend to have more impact on salary than the professional qualification you have gained.

A newly qualified accountant typically earns between £27,000 and £36,000, with an average salary of £31,500. Accountants in London and South-East England earn more, ranging from £38,000 to £50,000 with the average being £43,000. After three or four years, these salaries could rise to between £40,000 and £75,000, again depending on location and type of employer. These figures are for basic salaries and do not include additional benefits such as pension scheme contributions, health insurance or performance-related pay.

The salaries at the top of the range are most likely to be offered in the financial services sector, which includes banks and insurance companies as well as accountancy firms themselves, and in media and entertainment companies.

ROOM AT THE TOP?

If you are ambitious and want your career in accountancy to take you as far as you can possibly go, where should you be setting your sights?

The senior roles, responsibilities and job titles in accountancy, like the more junior ones, are not consistent between different employers but this summary will give you an idea of where you might aim for and how long it will take you to achieve your goal.

In firms

The most senior members of accountancy firms are the partners.

In a partnership arrangement, the partners are the owners of the firm and share responsibility for decisions on how it is run as a business. Partners also have ultimate responsibility for the work and the actions of the firm and its employees, which could mean that they could be personally liable for any debts or losses it incurs, or any fines or compensation that it might be ordered to pay as a result of professional negligence on the part of anyone in the firm. For many firms, if something like this were to happen the partners could be ordered to pay many millions of pounds out of their own resources and they have therefore restructured themselves as 'limited liability partnerships' (LLPs) – over half of the top 60 firms are now structured in this way. The partners still run the firm but their personal assets are not at risk from any business liabilities.

There are different types of partner with different levels of responsibility, depending on how the firm is structured.

Senior partner

The senior partner heads up the firm. In some firms, this may be a 'first among equals' post, acting as the public face and spokesperson of the firm, especially to clients, but with other members of the partnership having an equal share in the running of the firm. In other firms, this position may be a much more powerful role, similar to that of a company chairman.

In some firms, the senior partner is referred to as the 'managing partner', but this job title is not always equivalent to senior partner. A managing partner in a large firm may be one of a number of people with the same title and with equal status, each responsible for managing the firm in their geographical region, rather than the most senior member of the partnership.

It is possible to reach senior partner level by your mid-40s, or even early-40s.

Equity partner

Most partners have an 'equity' share in their firm: they have invested their own capital in it and their remuneration is based on the firm's performance. The firm's profits are divided equally between the partners, but many firms have more complex arrangements for sharing out the profits, based on factors such as individual performance or seniority.

Salaried partner

These have the 'partner' title and there is no outward difference between them and the equity partners. However, as they do not have a share in the firm they are still, in effect, employees. Their salary is fixed and does not go up or down according to how well or badly the firm does in any one year (although they may receive a bonus on top of their salary). A salaried partner position is often the first step to becoming an equity partner.

As well as managing the firm, partners represent it to clients. Each partner will have a group of clients for whom they are the first point of contact and they also work to bring in new clients by networking and by marketing the firm and its services.

Most people who are going to achieve partnership are likely to do so by their mid- to late-30s, although some high-fliers will be made partners in their late 20s.

Partners, especially in larger firms, have often gained some experience of working outside practice. An inside knowledge of industry and commerce is helpful to them when working with clients at a high level and gives their advice more weight. Experience of working outside the UK is another useful preparation for partnership in global firms and opportunities for overseas secondments are covered later in this chapter.

A junior partner in a Big Four firm can earn around £250,000 plus benefits. The average income of partners in these firms ranges from £500,000 to £900,000 with the most senior partners earning over £1 million a year. The partners' income is affected by their own performance as well as that of the firm overall, as these firms all have reward structures based on performance.

Partner income in small firms is very far below these levels. A partner in a small London firm may earn well below £100,000 – outside London their income would be still lower.

Greg Stevenson, partner, Knox Cropper.

Greg is one of five partners at his firm, which specialises in the not-for-profit sector and small business clients. He joined the firm as a trainee, following an archaeology degree at Southampton University, and became a partner in 2000.

'I didn't know what career I wanted to go into until my final year at university, but I had some relatives who were accountants and they suggested that this would be a good option. There seemed to be more opportunities for accountants than for archaeologists, and the pay was better too!

'It took me a number of years to qualify – the exam structure was quite different at that time and even harder to pass than it is now! Once I had qualified I became a supervisor, moving up to manager three years later and senior manager three years after that. At senior manager level, I became a fee earner with my own portfolio of clients, meaning that I was the main point of contact with the firm for these clients, and then became an equity partner in 2000 – 10 years after qualifying.

'My firm has a very strong focus on not-for-profit clients, such as charities, trades unions and housing associations. Accounting for these organisations involves a different approach – looking at income and resources rather than profits and losses – and a different set of accounting requirements from those that apply to businesses. I meet the chief executives and finance directors of these organisations to discuss their accounts and any issues arising from them before an audit is carried out and then, once the assignment is completed, present the accounts and my accompanying report to the trustees.

'My firm has three offices and I now divide my time between our London and Surrey offices. Most of the work in the London office is based around audit in the not-for-profit sector, while the Surrey office has a greater number of small businesses, trust and tax clients. I have more contact with these clients than I do with my not-for-profit clients, as a lot of the advice and support they need is ongoing. I usually meet audit clients a number of times a year but smaller clients, who use the firm for a number of different services such as payroll, preparing accounts and tax advice, I see more regularly.

'As a partner, I spend about 20% of my time on the management of the firm. This involves carrying out reviews to ensure that we are complying with all the relevant standards and regulations; review work in progress and costs and billing clients. The rest of my time is spent working directly with clients, providing advice, planning and managing the audit process, reviewing the work and reporting back to the client at the end of the process. Although my role now is to oversee audits rather than actually to take part in them, I still do find that some hands-on work is necessary.

'One of the best things about accountancy is being able to help people – especially the type of clients that my firm works with. They look to you for the professional help and advice that will make their role easier and benefit the work of their organisation. It's a good career and one that can always offer new possibilities.'

In industry and commerce

Again, job roles at the top of the profession carry a range of different job titles and responsibilities. Some of these are detailed below.

Finance director

This is the top of the accountancy tree outside practice. The finance director may alternatively be referred to as chief financial officer, depending on the preference of the company.

The finance director (FD) has a seat on the board of directors and works with fellow directors to decide how the company should operate, develop its business and respond to changes in its business environment. The FD has ultimate responsibility for the organisation's financial affairs, such as managing its cashflow, compliance and accounts, but also plays a full part in all other business decisions. In fact, the FD is usually regarded as one of the most senior members of the board and often acts as right-hand man (or, less commonly, woman) to the chief executive officer (CEO).

At this level, the FD's non-finance skills such as communication, negotiation and influencing are just as important as their accounting knowledge and experience.

The average basic salary for an FD of a FTSE 100 company in 2008 was £456,432 – but bonuses and other benefits meant that the average FD in these companies took home just over a million pounds that year. The FD with the highest total pay took home just over £2.7 million. Not all FDs are in this league, though, and a number of FDs of smaller listed companies earned around £50,000. The FDs of some of the UK's largest companies are in their mid-40s.

The FD may be at the top of the accountancy ladder but many FDs progress still further by leaving their specific financial role to take the next step up and become CEO themselves. The CEO is the most senior executive of the company with overall responsibility for its management and the FD role is a good preparation for this role for several reasons:

■ the finance function is an ideal way to see how all the different areas of a business fit together and contribute to the organisation as a whole

■ the close working relationship between an FD and their CEO, which gives the FD first-hand insight into the CEO's role

■ the skills needed in both roles are similar.

Almost one-third of the CEOs of FTSE 100 companies have a finance background.

Financial controller

Since the FD looks at the big picture, with responsibilities extending beyond pure finance, it is important that somebody should have responsibility for managing the day-to-day financial issues of the business – this is where the financial controller (FC) comes in. The FC will focus on the everyday details and manage the company's systems and procedures, keeping in close touch with the FD but freeing them up for their wider management role. A good FC is as important to their FD as a good FD is to the CEO and many do become FD themselves later in their career.

This role may, in companies where the top position in finance has the title of CFO, be given the title of finance director, so it is important not to confuse the two.

FCs would normally be expected to have at least five years' post-qualification experience and their salaries range from £45,000 to £90,000 – possibly even higher in certain industries and locations.

Job titles and career structures vary between different employers: Table 10 lists commonly-used titles in these sectors to give a general indication of possible steps on the career ladder.

There are also variations in the experience and qualifications sought at different levels: a 'semi-senior' or 'assistant management accountant' position, for example, may be open to part-qualified (PQ), newly-qualified (NQ) or more experienced accountants depending on the employer. The PQE column in this table is only a very rough guide to the level of experience that might be expected in these roles – some people will move up the ladder faster than others, meaning that there is a lot of overlap between these grades.

Table 10 Post-qualification career paths

Post-qualification experience (PQE)	Private practice	Industry and commerce	Public sector
10–15 years	Partner	Finance director	Director of finance
5–10 years	Senior manager	Financial controller	Deputy director
4–5 years	Manager	Finance manager	Assistant director

(Continued)

Post-qualification experience (PQE)	Private practice	Industry and commerce	Public sector
From 2–3 years PQE	Assistant manager	Senior management accountant Senior financial accountant	Head of section
NQ – 3–4 years PQE	Senior	Management accountant Financial accountant	Management accountant Financial accountant
PQ/NQ/1 year PQE	Semi-senior	Assistant management accountant Assistant financial accountant	Assistant management accountant Assistant financial accountant

In the public sector

Local authorities and many other public bodies, for some reason best known to themselves, tend to call their chief financial officers 'director of finance' rather than 'finance director'. The equivalent to a financial controller is normally known as the 'deputy director' and there may be one or more assistant directors. Inevitably, these titles are not standardised and they vary between different organisations.

Probably the most impressive title in accountancy is that of the head of the National Audit Office, who is known as the Comptroller and Auditor-General. This, though, is only an abbreviation of the even more impressive full title: Comptroller General of the Receipt and Issue of Her Majesty's Exchequer and Auditor-General of Public Accounts.

In a number of local authorities, the finance department has been merged with other corporate functions, giving directors of finance responsibility for areas such as administration and legal services as well as finance. This is also the case in many not-for-profit organisations, such as charities, which tend to have a much flatter management structure and fewer levels in the hierarchy.

The salaries of finance directors in the public sector may not reach the heights of their counterparts in business or in practice, but they do reach six-figure levels. In local government, they range from £110,000 to £135,000; a deputy can earn from £90,000 to £108,000. Salaries at a similar level of seniority in central government bodies range from £100,000 to £180,000.

Gareth is a former head of finance at the Royal Zoological Society of Scotland.

'I was always good at maths and for my sins did maths and further maths A levels. I didn't want to do a pure maths degree and decided to look at financial courses, finally selecting Accounting with Computing at the University of Kent where I graduated in 1980.

'I started off in London working for Thomson McLintock (who eventually became part of KPMG). I really enjoyed working there and gained lots of experience in auditing property, insurance, pension, food production and oil companies. I also worked on an investigation at a London casino – it was mind-blowing to see the amounts of money being gambled every day!

'I didn't fare so well on the exam front and failed a referral on my ICAEW part 1 exams. I decided to leave and move into industry so I joined BUPA, which had just set up a separate head office finance function for its hospital division. I managed to progress up the ladder without a formal qualification and became management accountant, responsible for co-ordinating the production of management accounts and information as well as the budgeting process. I spent a great deal of time travelling round to hospitals and nursing agencies, but this was a job that I loved.

'I relocated to Scotland when a vacancy arose in an independent hospital in Edinburgh where BUPA had a contract to run the hospital and provide the senior management team. As well as the finance function I also had operational responsibilities covering medical bookings, portering, customer service and general management.

'During this time I never got around to resitting any accounting exams but this didn't affect my career within BUPA. I did, however, gain an MBA from Edinburgh University in 1995.

'Unfortunately I was made redundant in 1999 following the implementation of a new IT system which centralised the finance function in Manchester. Within a month I was working as college accountant at Edinburgh University. It was during this time that I decided that I should buckle down and get qualified.

'The ACCA qualification appealed to me as it was modular and was also being taught by evening class at Napier University. I also felt that it covered more accounting issues than other accountancy qualifications and would offer me more career opportunities.

'Having gained my professional qualification after over 20 years in accountancy, I joined the Royal Zoological Society of Scotland in 2005. My role here was certainly different! The society is a registered charity that owns and operates Edinburgh Zoo as well as the Highland Wildlife Park near Aviemore. Like other zoos in the UK it does not receive any financial support from the public sector and has to generate its own resources through commercial activities, such as catering and retail, as well as admission charges.

'My role here was fairly hands-on, being the only qualified accountant on the staff. I was responsible for both finance and IT with six staff reporting to me. I provided advice to other departments and fully participated in the strategy of the society – for example, putting together a business plan based on introducing giant pandas into the collection.

'Finance in a charity is always interesting as the legislative requirements for charities are fairly strict – VAT is also complex due to partial exemption issues. So I learned a lot at the society – and no, the animals don't appear in the accounts as assets or stock, as zoos generally exchange animals at no cost.

'Although I was able to have a successful career for 20 years without becoming professionally qualified, I think that qualifications are really important now – the days of being able to move up the ladder if you are only "qualified by experience" are over. So work hard and get those exams over and done with! Then you can move on and build your skills and experience.'

OPPORTUNITIES OVERSEAS

The opportunity to spend some time working overseas is a big attraction for many people when they choose to apply to the big accountancy firms or to multinational companies. A few people may be able to do this during their training but for most accountants it is only once they qualify that this opportunity becomes a real possibility. The Big Four firms in particular offer secondments to their offices throughout the world and encourage their newly qualified staff to apply for these positions.

At this point, though, many people hesitate. Three years after joining the firm, they may have taken on commitments, such as buying a flat. They may now be in a steady relationship with someone who won't be able to come abroad with them because of their own work commitments. Even if they are free of all such ties, they may wonder how valuable their newly gained qualification will be outside the UK and whether, when they return from their stint overseas, they will find that they have been sidelined and will need to start climbing the career ladder all over again.

This particular worry isn't usually well founded, and experience abroad, gaining experience of another country and its business culture, is seen by many of the big firms as something that will enhance your career prospects in many ways. Many of the clients of these firms are themselves large multinational businesses and they will expect their advisers to have a similar global mindset to themselves.

The work itself may not be significantly different from that in the UK, especially in the Big Four firms who, as far as possible, have standardised their working practices and support structures in all their offices, wherever in the world they are located. Audit skills are relatively easy to transfer abroad due to the widespread use of IFRSs, which means that accountants need to work to the same standards in many different countries. Tax work may be more complex as there are significant variations in tax laws between different countries, but tax accountants with a UK qualification still can and do take up international secondments. It may be necessary, though, for them to spend longer periods of time abroad to allow them time to become familiar with a new set of legal principles and tax regulations.

Even though the work of accountants in different countries may be similar, there are still language and cultural differences that you will need to be prepared for and to adapt to. In countries such as Australia or the USA these may be minimal: other countries may present a greater challenge.

Some multinational employers use English as a common language throughout the organisation, allowing staff from many different countries to work together and to move around the organisation without needing intensive language training before they can do their job. In accountancy firms, while it may be possible to work through English in some non-English speaking countries, it is preferable to have a good knowledge of at least one other language as you will normally be expected to be able to work with clients in their own language. Employers will provide support for their staff to keep up their language skills, or to learn new languages, if this will be helpful to them in their work. Cultural awareness training and advice on business etiquette is also provided where necessary before staff go abroad.

Firms are now making greater efforts to keep their staff 'in the loop' while they are on a secondment – this can include regular reviews, maintaining regular contact with their 'home' office and planning how their experience outside the firm can be put to good use when they return.

A 2009 survey by the ICAEW found that chartered accountants who had had some international experience during their career commanded the highest salaries. While this may reflect the fact that the best opportunities for working on an international basis are to be found in the largest firms, who pay the highest salaries anyway, it still helps to show the value of some experience outside the UK.

The main thing to keep in mind when you are thinking about international experience is that it is not a holiday! Employers will offer international placements according to their business needs and these may not always be in the locations that you would choose to go to as a tourist. The fastest-growing countries, in all aspects of business, are China and Russia so, although relevant language skills would usually be needed to work in these locations, experience here could be particularly useful to enhance your career.

A GLASS CEILING?

Women are well represented in the accountancy profession: just under half of students training with the six chartered bodies are female and the proportion of qualified female members has risen steadily over the past five years, from 27% to 32%.

However, while a number of women have succeeded in reaching the highest levels in the profession (partner or finance director) it is, unfortunately, fair to say that these are still very much in a minority.

- Only two of the top 100 accountancy firms have female managing partners.

- Only 13% of partners in the top 50 firms are women.

- Only four of the FTSE 100 companies have a female finance director.

- Overall, women hold only around 10% of senior posts in accountancy.

This shortage of female role models in senior positions can lead to the perception that there is still a 'glass ceiling' blocking women's path to the top of the accountancy profession. While this would be an unfair exaggeration, women in accountancy do still, as in many other career areas, lag behind men in their career development and rewards.

The main reason for this is the issue of combining a career with family responsibilities. Until their early 30s, men and women earn very similar salaries, but from this point (the point at which women are most likely to have children) women's salaries fall sharply in relation to those of men as they take career breaks or reduce their working hours and responsibilities.

A high proportion of women working outside practice are employed in the not-for-profit sector, in public bodies and charities. These employers are the most likely to offer flexible working and family-friendly policies but also generally pay lower salaries than employers in the private sector.

A number of high-profile employers in the private sector are trying to improve work–life balance for their employees. This is, of course, something that can benefit any member of staff, male or female, whether or not they are parents, but some of these employers' schemes are particularly targeted at women. Employers do not want to lose good staff, especially if they have invested a considerable amount in their training and career development, so offering working hours and practices that fit in with employees' life outside the office benefits the employer as well.

Some of the women in high-level and high-profile roles in accountancy include Zarin Patel, the Chief Financial Officer of the BBC, Ruth Porat, CFO at investment bank Morgan Stanley and Sally O'Neill, Director of Finance at the Royal Opera House.

All of the Big Four firms, and many other large employers, offer flexible working and career development programmes to encourage more women to take up senior posts. They have introduced structured initiatives such as mentoring and leadership programmes as well as family-friendly initiatives such as flexible working and childcare allowances. Many companies have equality and diversity managers whose role is to ensure that no employee is disadvantaged in their career on the grounds of gender, race, disability, or any other factor that might give rise to unfair discrimination.

Some smaller employers, with few staff and working within tight budgets, may find it difficult to accommodate working parents in any way beyond what the law requires. Others, though, can find it easier than larger employers to make individual arrangements to help their staff fit their work around their families.

Not all women (or all men), though, will want to reach the top of their profession and accountancy offers many opportunities for contract or part-time work which are still reasonably well paid and can be conveniently fitted in around family life or any other responsibilities or interests outside work.

LIFE BEYOND ACCOUNTANCY

Accountancy itself offers a great variety of career paths, but for some people it can be a springboard to a completely different role. This doesn't have to mean moving to a different employer: the size of large accountancy firms means that they can provide many opportunities outside their core business of accountancy, while in-house accountants working with other functions in their company may be able to move sideways.

Some of the most common moves for accountants who change direction are listed below.

Human resource management

Many accountants who move into this area first get involved through training or recruitment, where their own experience can be directly put to use. Accountancy training, though, is not just concerned with technical accountancy skills. It also includes other practical skills such as computing and languages, plus 'soft skills' training, such as leadership and presentation skills, making it a very broad field of work. Recruitment can involve accountants in interviewing, giving presentations at schools, universities and careers events and organising internships.

Marketing

This may involve marketing an accountancy firm to clients or marketing an accountancy training scheme to students. Marketing has been defined as 'the business activity of presenting products or services to potential customers in such a way as to make them eager to buy'. Marketing the firm to a potential client, for example, would mean convincing the client that the firm can provide the quality and level of service they require at a price that fits their budget. Marketing involves activities such as: research; writing briefing documents; producing marketing materials such as websites, brochures and promotional items; and preparing and delivering presentations. A marketing campaign for a firm will draw on different aspects of an accountant's knowledge and experience depending on who the target of the campaign is – a pitch to gain the audit of a major PLC will require a very different approach, and a different type of knowledge, from running a stand at a graduate recruitment fair.

Management consultancy

Accountancy firms often describe themselves as 'business advisers' and management consultancy is all about advice, to both businesses and not-for-profit organisations, making accountancy qualifications and experience a good background for this career. In fact, four of the top 10 management consultancy firms are the consultancy divisions of the Big Four accountancy firms. A fifth, the top firm Accenture, originally formed part of the now-defunct accountancy firm Arthur Andersen.

Management consultancy has been defined as 'the provision to management of objective advice and assistance relating to the strategy, structure, management and operations of an organisation'. The insight that accountants have gained through their qualification and experience – whether in practice, industry or the public sector – helps to give them the knowledge and understanding that management consultants need. Good communication and people skills, though, are equally important.

Other possibilities

Accountants become MPs, sports promoters, journalists, lawyers and much more. There are even former accountants working as magicians and musicians!

Working for yourself

This doesn't just mean setting up your own accountancy firm – although many accountants do this. As an accountant in private practice, you will gain an insight into a variety of different businesses; in industry, you will get an in-depth knowledge of all the different areas of your employer's business. This business knowledge gives accountants a good foundation for running any kind of an entrepreneurial business, in areas from retail to restaurants and from pottery to property.

A book like this can only be an introduction to the range of possibilities that accountancy offers, giving a brief overview of the career paths, the routes to qualification and the work of accountants.

If you, like all good accountants, have an enquiring mind, you will probably still have many questions about accountancy and how to become an accountant.

Fortunately, there is a wealth of information on the internet about accountancy careers. In particular, the websites of the professional accountancy bodies will tell you about the qualifications they offer, how and where you can study and train for them and what the exams involve. These professional bodies, their websites and contact details are listed in Chapter 9.

The last word should go to some of the people profiled in this book: people who just a few years ago were, like you, in the process of choosing their career and are now positive that, in deciding on accountancy, they made the right choice.

> *Accountancy has exceeded my expectations – I am surprised by how much my knowledge and understanding of the economy and businesses has increased.*
>
> *David, Ensors*

Don't look on accountancy as boring bean-counting – it can be exciting, you will learn a lot from it and it gives a superb grounding for a business career, in whatever discipline you choose.

Matt, PKF

Give it a try! Do an internship or some work experience that will give you a feel for what accountancy is really like. It's hard work but definitely worthwhile.

Katie, PKF

Chapter Eight
FURTHER RESOURCES

WEBSITES

Accountancy Age

www.accountancyage.com

The website includes lists of the top 100 accountancy firms, news feeds, forums and information on specific areas within accountancy.

CareersinAudit.com

www.careersinaudit.com

Jobs board and careers resource with articles, tips and profiles.

Financial Services Skills Council

www.fssc.org.uk/directions

The Financial Services Skills Council (FSSC) is an independent, employer-led organisation which links finance sector employers, government and educational bodies to encourage education, training and skills development for financial services, accountancy and finance across the UK.

The FSSC's Directions website provides people interested in the financial services sector with careers information, job profiles and case studies covering a number of career areas, including accountancy.

Graduate Prospects

www.prospects.ac.uk

Graduate careers website which includes profiles of career sectors and jobs as well as a vacancy database.

Inside Careers

www.insidecareers.co.uk

Careers advice and employer information covering chartered
accountancy, management accountancy and tax advice.

Milkround

www.milkround.com

Graduate vacancy site which also includes background on careers and
employers

Target Jobs

http://targetjobs.co.uk

Site for graduates with careers advice, vacancies and background on
career sectors.

BOOKS

Houston, Kathleen, *Winning CVs for First-time Job Hunters*, Richmond:
Trotman Publishing 2008.

Houston, Kathleen, *Winning Interviews for First-time Job Hunters*,
Richmond: Trotman Publishing 2008.

Redman, Alan, *Practise and Pass Professional: Numeracy Tests*,
Richmond: Trotman Publishing 2010.

Redman, Alan, *Practise and Pass Professional: Verbal Reasoning Tests*,
Richmond: Trotman Publishing 2010.

Chapter Nine
USEFUL CONTACTS

Association of Accounting Technicians
140 Aldersgate Street, London EC1A 4HY
Tel: 020 7397 3002
Fax: 020 7397 3009
join@aat.org.uk
www.aat.org.uk

Association of International Accountants
Staithes 3, The Watermark, Metro Riverside, Newcastle upon
   Tyne NE11 9SN
Tel: 0191 493 0277
Fax: 0191 493 0278
recruitment@aiaworldwide.com
www.aiaworldwide.com

Association of Taxation Technicians
First Floor, 11–19 Artillery Row, London SW1P 1RT
Tel: 0844 251 0830
Fax: 0844 251 0831
info@att.org.uk
www.att.org.uk

Chartered Accountants Ireland
The Linenhall, 32–38 Linenhall Street, Belfast BT2 8BG
Tel: 028 9043 5840
Fax: 028 9023 0071
careers@charteredaccountants.ie
www.charteredaccountants.ie

Chartered Institute of Management Accountants
26 Chapter Street, London SW1P 4NP
Tel: 020 8849 2251
Fax: 020 8849 2450
cima.contact@cimaglobal.com
www.cimaglobal.com

Chartered Institute of Public Finance and Accountancy
3 Robert Street, London WC2N 6RL
Tel: 020 7543 5656
Fax: 020 7543 5700
students@cipfa.org.uk
www.cipfa.org.uk

Chartered Institute of Taxation
First Floor, 11–19 Artillery Row, London SW1P 1RT
Tel: 020 7340 0550
Fax: 0844 579 6701
education@ciot.org.uk
www.tax.org.uk

Consultative Committee of Accountancy Bodies
PO Box 433, Moorgate Place, London EC2P 2BJ
Tel: 020 7920 8405
admin@ccab.org.uk
www.ccab.org.uk

Financial Reporting Council
Fifth Floor, Aldwych House, 71–91 Aldwych, London WC2B 4HN
Tel: 020 7492 2300
www.frc.org.uk

Her Majesty's Revenue & Customs
100 Parliament Street, London SW1A 2BQ
www.hmrc.gov.uk

Insolvency Practitioners Association
Valiant House, 4–10 Heneage Lane, London EC3A 5DQ
Tel: 020 7623 5108
Fax: 020 7623 5127
secretariat@insolvency-practitioners.org.uk
www.insolvency-practitioners.org.uk

Institute of Certified Bookkeepers
1 Northumberland Avenue, London WC2N 5BW
Tel: 0845 060 2345
info@bookkeepers.org.uk
www.bookkeepers.org.uk

Institute of Chartered Accountants in England and Wales
Metropolitan House, 321 Avebury Boulevard, Milton Keynes MK9 2FZ
Tel: 01908 248040
Fax: 01908 248088
careers@icaew.com
www.icaew.com/careers

Institute of Chartered Accountants of Scotland
CA House, 21 Haymarket Yards, Edinburgh EH12 5BH
Tel: 0131 347 0161
Fax: 0131 347 0108
catraining@icas.org.uk
www.icas.org.uk

Institute of Internal Auditors
13 Abbeville Mews, 88 Clapham Park Road, London SW4 7BX
Tel: 020 7498 0101
Fax: 020 7978 2492
studentsupport@iia.org.uk
www.iia.org.uk

International Association of Bookkeepers
Suite 30, 40 Churchill Square, Kings Hill, West Malling ME19 4YU
Tel: 01732 897750
Fax: 01732 897751
mail@iab.org.uk
www.iab.org.uk

Network of Independent Forensic Accountants
Tel: 0845 609 6091
enquires@nifa.co.uk
www.nifa.co.uk

Voluntary Service Overseas
317 Putney Bridge Road, London SW15 2PN
Tel: 020 8780 7500
enquiry@vso.org.uk
www.vso.org.uk